MEMORY

Memory

Encounters with the Strange and the Familiar

JOHN SCANLAN

REAKTION BOOKS

To Morvern Callar . . .

Published by Reaktion Books Ltd
33 Great Sutton Street
London EC1V 0DX, UK

www.reaktionbooks.co.uk

First published 2013

Printed and bound in Great Britain
by Bell & Bain, Glasgow

A catalogue record for this book is available from the British Library.

ISBN 978 1 78023 178 5

Contents

INTRODUCTION 7

I
Pasts 17

II
Presences 60

III
Ecologies 109

CONCLUSION 155

REFERENCES 159
SELECT BIBLIOGRAPHY 177
ACKNOWLEDGEMENTS 181
PHOTO ACKNOWLEDGEMENTS 183
INDEX 184

INTRODUCTION

Contemporary life provides a fitting stage on which to unravel the seemingly immutable contradictions and complexities of human memory. To take one example, advocates of scientific research into the possibilities of seemingly infinite data storage would have us believe that whatever our anxieties about forgetting, or lacking the means to adequately and reliably record, or 'remember', the particulars of a world in motion, we can rest assured that the latest technological fix will allow us to leap into a new future in which human limits become increasingly irrelevant. In such circumstances it is always wise to take the temperature of current futurology, which offers – among much else – a fascinating insight into the new phenomenon of 'memory engineering', or 'the process of fashioning our inchoate digital pasts into useful memories'.[1] Digital memory, with which almost everyone reading this book will be familiar, is currently the subject of intense scientific activity aimed at uncovering the means by which it can be shrunk in physical terms while being expanded in its virtual storage capacity. It was recently revealed, for instance, that researchers at Harvard Medical School have now discovered the means to use DNA to store written data of the kind found in books, libraries and archives. 'One gram of DNA', it was reported, 'can hold 455 billion gigabytes; four grams could theoretically contain a year's worth of the entire world's data.'[2] Some commentators quickly suggested that before long, entire libraries which now take up great amounts of physical space could be stored in the fur of a family cat, or under a human thumbnail.

Why worry, then, about memory, when all that seems to remain is to find robust means of retrieving and reading its 'data'? One reason, perhaps, is that whatever revolutions in technology do to improve our lives, and to help us to store and retrieve vast quantities of information – with all that means for our ability to access a past that is always vanishing in front of our eyes – they do not overcome the social and cultural implications of our reliance on what is referred to as 'external memory' (that is, as distinct from the organic, biological entity). At around the same time as I was reading of the latest scientific breakthrough in DNA storage, I could not help noticing a large advert on the back of a bus for so-called 'memory pills'. 'Feed your mind', it read: 'for brain performance and memory'. Further investigation into these pills revealed a baffling array of such herbal supplements, which promise to 'boost memory', 'improve alertness and mental perform-ance' and 'help improve absent mindedness'. Despite the great techno-logical leaps that keep remaking 'memory', we still worry about the fact that ageing makes us forgetful – because at its worst, such forgetting collapses the entire basis of personal and social life.

Memory, it seems, provides us with the capacity for experiencing where we are in the temporal flow; it is our sense of where we belong, and how we relate and connect to others. As such, it provides us with the comfort of the familiar. Yet, at the same time, the fact that memory – the 'shifting and confused gusts' of fleeting duration famously explored in Marcel Proust's *In Search of Lost Time* – can undo our present sense of time and place, and thus remind us that

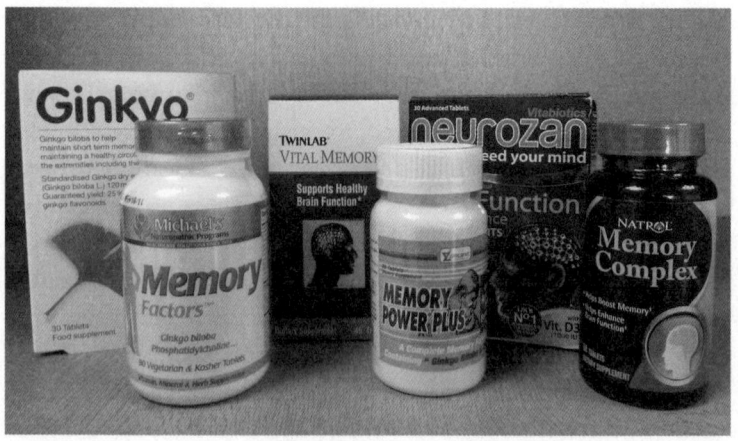

A selection of 'memory pills'.

we live also with the past, means that it is also often discomfiting and strange.[3] From a socio-cultural perspective – one necessarily informed by the philosophical history of memory – to grasp the centrality of memory to human life, and by extension to our contemporary world, is to understand how we are both at home in the world and estranged from it; to understand why being human is to negotiate and make sense of our encounters with the strange and the familiar.

Imagine you have no memory, no need or desire for recollection. You belong to the animal world and are at one with it, as it is at one with you. But it seems that to possess memory – which is also to be possessed by memory – is precisely to be capable of imaginative leaps beyond your present concerns. You might think of these as backwards perspectives that often appear to open up as if from nowhere, just as when you suddenly become conscious of objects appearing in the rear-view mirror as you drive forwards. Whatever memory is – a split in perceptual awareness, a rupture in the temporal flow, a virtual realm and so on – it is the means by which we are able to separate ourselves from the immediacy, the here-and-now, of existence; which is to say, from mere animality. Carried to the limit, this notion of self-consciousness moves us towards a kind of exile.

To have memory is – metaphorically speaking – to be thrown into the world, cast to the wind, and with an awareness of some temporal anterior. A life such as this implies – one that unfolds both backwards and forwards – is characterized by the meshing of temporalities. Philosophy and memory share this much in common: they derive their existence from the self-awareness or self-consciousness of how time and experience take us far from our origins while, at the same time, that very experience roots us in the world. 'All philosophy', as the German poet and philosopher Novalis wrote in the late eighteenth century, 'is homesickness'.[4] It seeks, in innumerable ways, to comprehend how our thinking produces a sense of being out-of-joint with our environment, our history. Thus philosophical thinking, Nietzsche agreed, was 'not so much a discovering as a recognizing, a remembering, a return and home-coming to a far-off, primordial total household of the soul'.[5]

Yet one might say that the memory that seems to reappear from that past as recollection (involuntary, as opposed to the willed efforts of remembering) intervenes as a kind of mythical temporality: a time out of time. Thus for most of us, as we carry on down our own little merry way, there will appear surprises, interruptions, openings – a doubling of existence that temporarily arrests perception, and which might produce the sensation of 'a kind of permanent homesickness' that directs us towards 'a compulsive stance of *spectatorship* over against the world'.[6] Here you are . . . but *there* you are; as in a flashback in which you sense yourself to be both subject and viewer of a private film that mirrors something that is both strange and familiar. As you become aware of it as an internal sensation – we might call it longing, nostalgia, déjà vu – the separation of past time and present space seems almost to vanish. The real world, for a moment, dissolves. Such impressions may present themselves as routes into shady and mysterious scenarios that open up and call us forth, no matter how unwelcome their appearance might be. Or perhaps what manifests itself as a doubling of existence becomes apparent through tokens or fetishes, souvenirs and mementoes, which are the keys that unlock past and present and work us over. It is arguably the case that an existential split defines modern experience in a more thoroughgoing way that it did in any earlier time, simply because the past, and knowledge of the past, is accumulated so comprehensively through archives and media, and through the preservation of physical traces. 'Hieroglyphic' was how Walter Benjamin described the topography of modern life; we occupy a space alive with treasures that could reveal the depth of history and the mysteries of a present easily bamboozled by its own everydayness.

For those who see the past as the source of powerful forces that merely lie dormant – and Walter Benjamin was one of them – we must pay attention to its fleeting appearances, which can be as elusive as flashes of lightning. The figure of the flâneur, who took up much of Benjamin's attention, was viewed as a proto-detective figure with an intuitive grasp of the fact that back *there*, and down *below*, there was something more. The depth of modern life was, in fact, memory:

> The street conducts the flâneur into a vanished time. For
> him, every street is precipitous. It leads downward – if not
> to the mythical Mothers, then into a past that can be all the

more spellbinding because it is not his own, not private. Nevertheless, it always remains the time of childhood ... In the asphalt over which he passes, his steps awaken a surprising resonance.[7]

Benjamin was convinced that the dead were all around us in the material stuff of modern life. This demanded a knowledge that could only be born of a 'telescoping of the past through the present'; the redemption of a collective memory that seemed to have been abandoned to progress and its new social forms and technologies, its media and its attachment to life at the surface.[8] Benjamin's fascination with memory lies in the interplay of surface and depth. This book seeks to show that in contemporary life, collective memory, as Benjamin understood it, is transformed. Without depth, we are not merely left with surface, but with a new ecology that abolishes the distinction – it is, rather, 'Surf Life' – not merely surface, but surfeit: a 'too-muchness' that defines the ecology of memory today. Benjamin's sense that fragments, ruins and small things are the key to larger truths – itself reflecting a variant of Leibniz's theory of monads (the idea that particulars, or monads, reflect a universality) – seems to be borne out in the present, when all around us, in our ambient networked spaces, infinite remembrance of some kind is at the behest of any wandering attention that stops to plunge in. It is no longer best thought of, however, as down there, underneath; but rather, out there in the atmosphere.

This kind of understanding of memory – as a phenomenon that surrounds us, that exists as a kind of knowledge that is already there if only we looked – harks back to the Platonic idea of anamnesis, or the belief that recollection is the repossession of truth. The object of this recollection, in Plato, was 'an atemporal reality which the soul is able to contemplate outside of the time of human life'.[9] Words like 'soul' and ideas of a remembering of that which is already known may not be too attuned to our contemporary ways of looking at life. In fact, we more probably think of memory as something rather different: to do with the mind, or the brain, or the self as a distinctive, individuated entity. This latter idea represents a different strand of modern thinking that runs through the development of psychology to the sciences of the mind. But, like the idea of collective memory we find in, for instance, Walter Benjamin, it might equally be traced to ancient antecedents.

One might point as far back as Aristotle, who observed that 'memories that are many in number form a single experience.'[10] Today we refer to such a unifying principle as the self. For Aristotle, what made you uniquely you was the outcome of experience; which is to say, you were the just the *experiences* you had (the events you lived through, the relationships and encounters that marked your life and so on), which are all tied together by memory. Memory was, then, the name for both your self-knowledge of these individual experiences, and for experience *in total*.

This relation of the individual to the empirical world – the fact that what you knew of yourself inside, so to speak, was connected to the world outside you – means that memory is experience that exists in time; experience that has a sense of its own past as being unique to itself.[11] This is illustrated, for instance, in autobiographical memory – recollection – which, in a sense, gathers up experience and attempts to provide it with some kind of unity. Thus for Montaigne, the originator of the personal, confessional essay, 'the very writing of the *Essays*' sees memory adding 'a sense of narrative coherence over time for the self, especially when its active, reconstructive moment is foregrounded'.[12] Such efforts to draw past experience into a self-identical form encapsulated a view of the self that was common to many modern philosophers, such as John Locke, who saw that we often lose touch with the continuity of our past selves. For Locke, Jan Goldstein notes,

> sheer absorption in present thoughts momentarily obliterates our awareness of our past selves; once a day consciousness itself is suspended in sleep. Hence memory must be enlisted to fill in the gaps and restore that continuity of consciousness called self.[13]

Without memory, after all, what would be left of a person? 'Everything is in a perpetual vicissitude', Diderot wrote in the century following Locke's formulation of the modern self, 'and I myself am never in one moment what I was in another'.[14] It was only memory that could unite the individual who was subjected to all of the alterations of time and age, yet could still emerge from the process recognizably the same to itself and others. As Jerrold Seigel notes, the *gradual* nature of physical change (Diderot wrote: 'like a swarm of bees, it is still the same entity because its parts are never replaced all at once') offered, for Diderot, 'part of the explanation for this persistence of identity'.[15]

The continuity of memory as a condition of self might also be revealed by contrasting it with states of being which are riven by flashes of mood and feeling that can overtake that very sense of subjective order and unity – existential dispersals that cause one to take leave of the senses that establish the self in terms of its temporal, autobiographical reach into a personal narrative. This 'kind' of memory – as distinct from the kind of recollection or emotional reverie made famous in Marcel Proust's *In Search of Lost Time* – therefore seems not to be 'passionate' (unless we view wilful forgetting as somehow constitutive of memory, too). 'The passions', Philip Fisher argues, are vehement and 'involve the most complete identification of the self with its momentary state'. An angry man, for instance, is beset most of all by a kind of amnesia that for a brief period may be all-consuming, primordial; he 'forgets that he has not always been angry with this person, that he will someday be beyond anger'.[16] Thus

> the unique grip of the present vehement state, in its thoroughness . . . undoes the very meaning of that modern notion of the self first found in Locke, where my integrated memory of my own earlier states makes up my identity in my own reflections.[17]

In a more general sense, if you don't have the ability to remember in this sense of remembrance being the core of self-identity, you have fallen out of time and would therefore find it impossible to do more than live in a continual present. This was illustrated recently by the case of 'EP', a man suffering from one of the most extreme forms of amnesia resulting from brain damage, whose predicament represents how dependent we are, as selves, on memory:

On a typical morning, EP wakes up, has breakfast, and returns to bed to listen to the radio. But back in bed, it's not always clear whether he's just had breakfast or just woken up. Often he'll have breakfast again, and return to bed to listen to some more radio. Some mornings he'll have breakfast a third time.[18]

A personal sense of time (as distinct from the historical sense of time) was for Aristotle the chief characteristic that bestowed the faculty of memory with its great powers.[19] We may think, for instance, of the relation that pertains between memory and the development of a sense of self-identity in young children. The child only develops a sense of *self* when it first begins to recognize its own appearance in a mirror, or within surroundings that are familiar; which is to say, when memory begins to structure consciousness of the world the child occupies. Memory, in a sense, becomes evident as the world that is reflected back at us.

Without getting into questions of how neuroscience understands memory – which are concerned with how the mind works, rather than the more cultural and philosophical issue of what memory is and how it relates to the human condition, which concern us – we can nonetheless observe that the inability to recognize oneself in relation to others, and to see how one's identity is bound to others, is a characteristic common to people suffering from degenerative disorders of the mind, such as Alzheimer's disease. Those who suffer such a loss of self – and here we may draw a rough analogy with the pre-self-conscious child – often reach a point, for instance, when they no longer recognize their own reflection when they look in a mirror. What they see, rather, is not themselves, but a stranger or someone other – possibly a known or misrecognized person, but from some other place or other time – looking back at them. Memory, on this level, is a great concern not only for people who are ageing and their families, but for medical science, and for healthcare systems and insurers who face numerous challenges that are effectively the result of the physical body outlasting the mind.

But just as the new 'sciences of memory' – including neurology and other experimental studies of the mind – were, in the words of Ian Hacking, 'rewriting the soul', thinkers more engaged with philosophical concerns could not help but echo the questions that had, since the ancient Greeks, occupied those who sought to describe what it meant to be human.[20] Thus speculation on memory is often what follows from considering the fate of the human in a changing world. For Nietzsche, indeed, life was 'structured by a dialectic of memory and amnesia, temporality and atemporality, being and becoming'.[21] To consider the first of those oppositions is also to recognize how much we derive from the oldest known attempts to understand how central memory was to the human condition.

The point at which memory and oblivion, or forgetting, become most associated with each other in the myths of ancient Greece – which give us so much of our idea of cultural memory, its vocabulary and existential dimensions – was at the boundary between this world and the next; between life and death. It was there that memory (Mnemosyne) and oblivion or forgetting (Lethe) assume, according to Jean-Pierre Vernant, the function of 'complementary religious powers', whose reach can perhaps teach us much about the peculiarities of cultural memory in our own time.[22]

Before crossing over into the world of the dead, a voyager 'was taken to two springs named Lethe and Mnemosyne':

> He drank from the first and immediately forgot everything about his human life, and, like a dead man, entered the realm of the Night. The water of the second spring enabled him to remember all that he had seen and heard in the other world. When he returned he was no longer restricted to knowledge of the present moment: contact with the beyond had revealed both past and present before him.[23]

We avoid forgetting by seeking the familiar, by developing a habitat – a home – that might overcome the sense of separation from the past. But we are against time, which does not 'stay awhile'. It is the accumulated shocks, departures and distances travelled by a modern self-consciousness that pairs remembering most obviously with its other, forgetting. 'Forgetting', Paul Ricoeur suggests, 'is the emblem of the vulnerability of the historical condition taken as a whole.'[24] If the modern human condition is to be thrust into historical time, it is this that makes memory – in cultural terms – what it is, what it has been. And so we remember or recollect what is not present, but always from a point in that present time and place. We are 'now-voyagers' – voyagers, that is to say, not into a distant past, but of a present that lights on to the past.

*

TO ADDRESS THE QUESTION of memory, as Matt K. Matsuda argues, is to venture into 'treacherous terrain'.[25] No work whose limits are as circumscribed as the present one could hope to give more than a sense of a phenomenon that seems, more than anything else, to define what it is to be human: because, in a sense, memory gives form to everything human that has been thought worthy of repetition or preservation, or at least that which has been required for the maintenance of life. And it is much more than what is visible or identifiable as 'memory'; it comes to be in everything we tinker with, extend ourselves into the world with, in order to make it more amenable to our needs, more 'homely'.

Keeping in mind, as one scholar argued, that the appearances of the word 'memory' 'are so numerous and its apparent meanings so legion that it would take the work of a lifetime to begin disentangling them', this book attempts to examine how we have come to live with and *within* 'memory'.[26] In particular it looks at the reasons ideas of home and habitat help us to understand the ways in which the nature of memory as an historical, technological and collective phenomenon is continually remaking everyday life; and why everyday life in turn identifies memory as an entity that forms part of a greater 'ecology' that is best understood in terms of remembering and forgetting.

I

Pasts

Memory does this: makes things small . . .
Land of the sailor.
Walter Benjamin

To consider memory as a peculiarly modern phenomenon is to reflect first of all on what it means to be human in a time of apparent separation, loss and trauma, and what we can say about life lived in a world in which experience no longer offers the comfort of predictable, cyclical time and the order of an immutable social hierarchy. It would be misleading to think solely in terms of a common modern assumption – of memory as the singular quality or characteristic that seemed most of all to guarantee a sense of personal identity, or some existential unity between self, past and present – to the exclusion of considerations about how the impersonal past also gives shape to our lives.

If we think of our own personal memory 'events', it seems clear that in both those occasions when we actively try to remember and in those when we are subject to recollections that wash over us without any effort on our part, we are establishing a connection to the past. Yet no past belongs to any individual alone: its sources are far more diffuse and more numerous than our everyday ways of talking and thinking about memory may allow. In this respect, who we are and where we come from seems to become more complex the instant we stop and think about it, just because we do so from a particular point in the present.

Home

Leaving aside the way that the past is refracted through the present, consider what 'inheritance' can mean in merely cultural terms. 'As *Homo sapiens* we are born of our biological parents', Robert Harrison has written; we are inheritors of genes – which we often think of as carriers of biological memory – but what such an observation leaves out is the continuity of the human condition as a self-consciousness of origins that touch more upon the notion of what it is to be at home in the world than the idea of mere biological existence (devoid of memory and sentiment) provides.[1] Thus 'as human beings we are born of the dead':

> of the regional ground they occupy, of the languages they inhabited, of the worlds they brought into being, of the many institutional, legal, cultural, and psychological legacies that, through us, connect them to the unborn.[2]

But, as well as the peculiarity of this human legacy, we also need to pay attention to the ways in which our lives are temporally extended. Occupying the present, we move backwards and forwards, at once seeming to both make and unmake the world, as Martin Heidegger's notion of *Dasein* and its 'ecstases' of being implies.[3] Echoing the well-known dictum of the eighteenth-century German poet and philosopher Novalis, that philosophy itself is just a desire 'to be everywhere at home', Heidegger thought that this multitemporal being – *Dasein* – sets out from a point of uncertainty in search of what he described as 'being as a whole':

> We are torn back by something, resting in a gravity that draws us downwards. We are underway to this 'as a whole'. We ourselves are this underway, this transition, this 'neither the one nor the other'.[4]

This 'whole' that draws us back in search of what we might suppose are origins was, for Heidegger, connected to truth as the making-apparent of something that had been concealed or forgotten about. That to which we have become oblivious nonetheless causes us 'to founder in the wake' of the concealment.[5] And that, we could say, is the nature of our estrangement: an awareness that the more distant these origins are, the more apparent the inevitability of death and the more certain the knowledge that we can never really be at home.

The pursuit of such a truth, though, was what Friedrich Nietzsche had dismissed as both the cause and the object of philosophy's atavism and nostalgia: philosophical knowledge was 'not so much a discovering as a remembering', he remarked, as it was always implicitly 'a return and home-coming to a far-off, primordial total household of the soul'.[6]

With a characteristic lack of sentimentality, Nietzsche – the anti-philosopher – also presumed himself to be immune from the effects of modernity and of the devastating consequences of progressive time on life, which left only forgetting, or the oblivion of the present-minded. Thus the past would have no claim on him as a 'memory' of origins that had long been lost. Instead, as Fredric Jameson observed, the Nietzschean view of the past when read (as it is) as a prescription for how we might live with the present, leaves us with something that seems devoid of memory, namely 'the deep bottomless vegetative time of *Being* itself, no longer draped and covered with myth or inherited religion'.[7]

To be thrust into a future that was not chosen – to be torn, as people were, from the life of tradition and from the security of a time immemorial – was also to be cut adrift, and perhaps left unaware that to be 'born of the dead' established the past as something that was not necessarily foreign, but as a continuity that also connects us to the unborn in a way that establishes a different, perhaps more moral context for our understanding of what a belonging that was at once multitemporal and theoretically homeless might be. The modern condition, though, was to 'forget as quickly as possible', and thus to have memory and history remake the past, often as something strange.[8] In the 'Land of the sailor', as Walter Benjamin would have it, what we see or remember may appear distant, in a shrunken state – yet still it draws us towards it.

But this feeling of separation or longing for some half-remembered home that has been seen to be so characteristic of philosophical thinking about the human condition in fact pre-dates philosophical reflection.[9] It is found first within the framework of the mythical thought of the ancient Greeks, and in the figure of Odysseus, who breaks the hold of myth and enters historical time, thus giving birth to an idea of memory that has persisted within the Western tradition to this day.[10]

Homer's *Odyssey* offers an early account of nostalgia – or, to use Benjamin's words, the view from the 'land of sailors' – retold as a song of loss and recovery in which a desire for home draws memory towards the gravitational pull of the homeland. In Edith Hall's account of the influence of the *Odyssey* on Western culture, she suggests that while there may have been similar poems pre-dating Homer which recounted tales of heroic returns home, the *Odyssey* is 'the only one that has survived to make its voyage across time and thus become the archetypal story of absence and return'.[11] Following Homer's epic, the idea of the journey home, returning to the innermost soul of one's being, comes to be known as the *nostos* – Greek for the mythical return. It is from this word that our own modern term 'nostalgia' emerges (with the addition of the medical suffix '-algia') in the seventeenth century. Before embarking on his long journey home, we see Odysseus trapped on the island of Calypso, where he sits by the shore daily, disconsolately 'looking out across the barren sea' as he dreams of a future that will reconcile him with the past in the homeland, and all the time 'tormenting himself with tears and sighs and heartache'.[12]

In a well-known account by Adorno and Horkheimer this desire to return home, which ultimately causes Odysseus to break the hold of fate over his life, forms part of 'a genealogy of modern self-enlightened reason'.[13] In their exploration of the fate of the idea of progress, enlightenment promises the dissolution of the kind of mythical world found to be characteristic of the archaic tradition, but nonetheless delivers itself up to its own myth of an all-conquering and immanent reason. Progress, in a sense, is always accompanied by its own counter-agent: by forces and tendencies that work to undo or negate the idea of progress as the liberation of humanity. The story of Odysseus becomes important for understanding the nature of cultural memory for a variety of reasons. In allowing the claim of memory to lead him back to his origins, for instance, the wily and ingenious Odysseus breaks apart the deterministic universe (or *mythos*), thus emerging as a self-conscious historical individual, a 'proto-bourgeois' figure, as Adorno and Horkheimer see it, emblematic of the drive towards self-mastery and the domination of nature that is a characteristic of enlightened reason and its drive to conquer all.[14] While this account and a variety of commentaries on it focus mainly on the relationship between the idea of enlightenment and, for instance, the rise of instrumental rationality, or reason's drive towards a kind of totalization that would remove life in its entirety from the grip of the irrational, what interests us here is simply that Odysseus leaps out of myth and into history. He leaps into historical being, which is to say, into a self-awareness of existing in a temporality that is both forward-moving and finite. In choosing a human fate rather than the immortality offered by his captor, Calypso, his example under-scores the idea of memory as both a separation of past from present, and possibly the means to bridge the two. He comes into a temporality, in other words, which contradicts the mythic time of eternal and immemorial cycles of ever-the-same.[15] The modern only makes sense when it is set against the archaic as something that overturns a mythical temporality. Nostalgia's lost object, whatever form it might take, is thus 'dependent', as Svetlana Boym argues, 'on the modern conception of unrepeatable and irreversible time'.[16]

By contrast with our own experience of time, the mythical did not progress into a future that was yet to be written; indeed, rather like the closed universe of a contemporary computer game, the actors are mere playthings of the gods, who determine that events unfold in a manner that repeats the same patterns over and over again. This makes individuals within the mythos 'figures of compulsion' who are 'programmed always to do the same thing'.[17] The salutary example we find in the *Odyssey* is in the encounter with the Sirens, the shore of whose island is littered with the bones of helpless sailors who had fallen into their trap. All sailors – until Odysseus, we learn – who always long to be at home and have had to pass the island of the Sirens have been seduced into their own demise by the lure of home. The power of the Sirens is in their ability to reflect whatever reminds the voyager most of home; it is thus that they sing 'from the listener's own place'.[18]

For Peter Sloterdijk, in the first instalment of a three-volume 'medial poetics of existence', *Spheres*, the Sirens' song is drawn out into an account of how we are always in search of a way back to some-thing that might offer the comfort of the mother's womb:

FRANCISCI DE VERULAMIO, Summi Angliæ Cancelarij, Instauratio magna.

Multi pertransibunt & augebitur scientia.

LONDINI Apud Joannem Billium Typographum Regium.

Anno 1620.

Hans Blumenberg writes that in Dante's reworking of the Homeric myth, Odysseus does not 'return home to Ithaca but rather takes the final adventure of crossing the boundary of the known world', whose gateway is represented by the Pillars of Hercules. As presented here, on the title page of Francis Bacon's *Instauratio magna*, the 'fateful boundary' of the pillars 'are already being transcended by shipping traffic', illustrating modern knowledge's progress into uncharted waters, leaving behind the world of myth.

> All truth-seekers . . . strive for what *prima facie* seems unattainable: they wish to tie the end of the search to the beginning of life and reverse birth through radical struggles against themselves. Who is the hero with a thousand faces if not the seeker who journeys out into the wide world in order to return home to his ownmost cave? The tales of heroic truth-seekers celebrate the womb immanence of all being.[19]

The Siren voices are thus akin to the voice of the mother, and of a kind of anamnesis – or, in other words, a remembering of all you have done, all you have been and the place to which you belong – that is attuned to the sense of the one cast adrift. Hand in hand with this all-encompassing remembering, the song the Sirens sing produces a kind of oblivion of being itself – a narcotic pull into forgetting the task at hand – to which those who are unprepared will surrender in order to hear the comforting song of heroic deeds and other events that mirror the soul, the remembrance, of the listener. In myth it is an encounter whose inevitable end is death, as the goddess Circe warns Odysseus.

After blocking up the ears of his own men to ensure they will not be diverted from their course by the sound of the deadly song, Odysseus chooses to hear the Sirens, and their song draws him in and weakens his resolve. But, tied to the mast of the ship so that he is unable to steer in the direction of the Sirens and fulfil their wish, his temporarily deafened men ignore his attempts to free himself as he has ordered, and they steer on through the danger.

In this encounter the song that proves so alluring attempts to seduce by recounting all that was great and admirable about Odysseus, almost as if the Sirens had the power to cause their victims to recollect the events that were closest to their hearts. In singing a song that offers the comfort of the mother's voice, and thus of the home that the voyager wishes to return to, accompanied by knowledge of 'whatever happens on this fruitful earth', the Sirens seem to hold the fate of Odysseus in the balance.[20] In breaking free of this fate, he alone finds a way out of the determined universe and gains control of his future. It is the journey of the hero back to his past that marks a 'central moment of enlightenment in myth'.[21] That moment, or opening, is the self-conscious leap out of mythical time and into history that, in modernity, we associate with the self, the 'I', the modern autonomous subject, and thus with something akin to personal memory as its unifying principle, as opposed to the remembrance of a past already written. Memory, in the example of Odysseus, thus transforms an unwanted fate into a series of events dominated by 'the supremacy of the subject', which, Hans Blumenberg argues, marks a turning point in the understanding of human experience, and one in which history overtakes myth.[22] 'The many mortal perils' Odysseus encounters and overcomes, Adorno and Horkheimer write, confirm for him 'the unity of his own life' and his 'identity as an individual'.[23]

> The opposition of enlightenment to myth is expressed in the opposition of the surviving individual ego to multifarious fate. The eventful voyage from Troy to Ithaca is the way taken through the myths by self – ever physically weak as against the power of nature, and attaining self-realization only in self-consciousness.[24]

The key point, though, is that memory as a condition of being proceeds from loss, and is therefore a product of self-consciousness. We might also understand this voyage from fate to self-mastery in terms of Hegel's description of the movement from consciousness to self-consciousness in *The Phenomenology of Spirit*, a transition which identified consciousness in terms of its 'own sense of inadequacy' or, we might equally say, its awareness of what it had lost, which for Hegel represented, Harvie Ferguson argues, 'nothing other than the advent of modernity'.[25]

The modern world is thus 'a world of separation and of pain' marked by a consciousness of 'a constitutive unhappiness', which again can be seen in terms of philosophy's homesickness, or yearning to return to a world of unbroken tradition. Yet it is against the uncertainties of modernity that we assert ourselves as the unique possessors of selves whose continuity seems guaranteed by the apparently unifying power of memory:

> This world not only has a consciousness of itself and the experience of this consciousness . . . it is because the world undergoes itself as a world of separation that its experience takes the form of the 'self'.[26]

In overcoming the world that opposes it, self-consciousness (Hegel's *Geist*, 'spirit') confronts its potential as 'a reality other than its own'. The modern individual, in other words, becomes aware of the doubling of existence:

> And self-consciousness, by behaving as a being-for-itself, aims to see itself as another independent being. This primary End is to become aware of itself as an individual in the other self-consciousness, or to make this other into itself.[27]

In other words, for Hegel, we project ourselves into a future that is always becoming, and thus always essentially self-negating. As modern men and women, we make a leap into the events that will shape our lives, attempting – so to speak – to coincide with ourselves, yet we trail a shadow or encumbrance, much like one of the human figures pictured in Étienne-Jules Marey's late nineteenth-century chronophotographs. There is always an implied forgetting in such movement, which boldly attempts to shrug off the garb of a previous existence. The past, however, is not so easily detached.

Hence the life of 'spirit', Hegel writes, is 'not the life that shrinks from death and keeps itself untouched by devastation, but rather the life that endures it and maintains itself in it'.[28] Those words, indeed, could be a description of the trials of Odysseus. Nonetheless, the singularity of this heroic, mythical figure, and the importance accorded to the homecoming in understanding the human condition even today, is there in the fact that Odysseus had leapt into another experiential dimension whose temporality is recognizably modern, which is is to say, self-defining. The others we encounter in such myths are like infants, acting out a course that has been laid before them in a manner that precedes what we know as self-identity. Such a fate, as we have seen, is the condition that Odysseus makes a break from, much in the manner of the 'leaping character' of the Hegelian dialectic that describes the birth of modernity.[29]

In the introduction to *The Phenomenology of Spirit* Hegel employs a more concrete example, with less abstract language, to underscore the nature of the movement from consciousness to self-consciousness. Just as a baby is born with the first breath 'after a long period of silent nutrition', which breaks, Hegel argues, 'the gradualness of merely continuing growth', consciousness ultimately arrives just as decisively, in 'a flash which all at once erects the structure of the new world'.[30]

But where Odysseus, the proto-modern individual, is able to engineer his return back to the homeland of Ithaca, the modern, Hegelian 'spirit' persists in loss. Yet it never loses its appetite for this archaic wholeness. Thinkers like Ferdinand Tönnies thought that the transition from premodern community to modern society left us in a state of exile, forever cut loose from the familiar and homely.[31] Even an unsentimental thinker like Karl Marx would contrast modernity with earlier epochs – the classical world in particular – and refer to the 'beautiful childhood' forever lost, and necessarily lost, that still exercises an 'eternal charm' over us.[32]

The fate of memory is bound to this self-consciousness, condemned to encounter its own becoming as it forever moves forward in an attempt at completion or self-reconciliation, yet always on the verge of plunging into a vertigo of undoing. As Jean-Luc Nancy argues, whatever in Hegel's account of the progress of self-consciousness

> might seem like a homecoming and an Odyssey of the universal spirit . . . should be immediately given the lie by this: on the one hand, the return is made nowhere else than to the depth, to the hollow of existence, and on the other, there is no Ulysses, no single and substantial figure of the subject.[33]

Why this becomes important to our discussion here is that it helps us to understand how self-consciousness itself produces a peculiarly modern kind of memory that is driven by both the urge for self-identity (a leap forwards) and by the dismantling power of the past in the form of recollection, reminiscence and, indeed, history – as a kind of quasi-memory of Hegel's self-conscious world. But the message for a contemporary understanding of memory is clear, too: as we travel backwards and forwards, projecting ourselves into becoming by some kind of leap into the future, it is in an act of self-making that is also at the same time an unmaking.

Unforgetting 27-40

But it is not only the individual who is assumed to be autonomous in this new modern world. While the human experience is remade as a *historical* experience – which is to say, an awareness of being in time and caught in events that, as Marshall Berman said, pour us 'into a maelstrom of perpetual disintegration and renewal' – that is not yet to speak of the practice of history as the study of the past.[34] Yet history's origins and its relation to what some would call 'memory' are somewhat similar in that they are rooted in this leap into the present, which reveals something now foreign in its wake.

Merely with respect to the definition of terms, the *modern* world separates itself from the past, but at the same time creates that past as a displaced anteriority; as, perhaps, a vague memory of traditions lost and thus an entirely new kind of historical object. But how does history become similarly autonomous, creating – in its act of distancing from the past which it makes its object – a kind of memory? Significant ruptures, such as the French Revolution and the onset of industrial society, represented a shift in historical consciousness at the level of everyday life, but also in the beginnings of disciplinary knowledge about past cultures and societies. Such events led ultimately to a sense of the past as something that ought to be preserved, which would create a curatorial impulse that continued to gather momentum right up to the present, in which we, in contemporary societies, live, in a culture defined by a mania for preservation.

In the eighteenth and nineteenth centuries a growing interest in the ruins of ancient civilizations and the development of academic fields such as archaeology, as well as history – whose object of interest reached from the more recent past to antiquity – established the value of the past.[35] The long-disputed Elgin Marbles, for instance, sculptured reliefs from the Acropolis of Athens, were held to be the common

The Elgin Marbles, fragments from the Acropolis of Athens acquired by Lord Elgin between 1801 and 1805, on display in the British Museum, London.

heritage of European civilization, and not merely of what had become of the Greek nation by that time.

The significance of Odysseus in all this is of course symbolic. What is important is the nature of his 'experience'. His exile from, and nostalgia for, the homeland allowed him to psychologically enter something common to the experience of modern society; for him, it was a kind of temporal crack in his fatalistic cosmos. For us it is the dawning of self-consciousness. His sense of loss and the memory of Ithaca, then, drive his journey to self-realization. He chooses mortality over immortality when offered the choice by Calypso.[36] In returning home, though, Odysseus was – in an important sense – journeying not back to his origins, but into the future, and in a way loosening himself from the grip of the past.

The shape of the ancient cosmos meant that what he left behind was a different notion of the past than the one we think of now as history's object of interest. Contrary to modern conceptions of memory which posit a lost – perhaps unrecoverable – anteriority, the past in ancient Greek thinking was always immanent, or, Jean-Pierre Vernant notes, 'an integral part of the cosmos' of the everyday world. Thus to confront the past was to come face-to-face with the depths of one's own being.[37] And as Vernant and Blumenberg, among others, have argued, the ancient *logos* that developed through the work of the Greek philosophers did not supplant the belief in myth but existed alongside it.[38]

> History as sung by Mnemosyne is a deciphering of the invisible, a geography of the supernatural . . . By removing the barrier that separates the present from the past, [memory] creates a bridge from the world of the living to the beyond, to which everything that leaves the light of day must return.[39]

Mnemosyne, the goddess of memory and mother of the Muses, those other figures of memory, personifies memory as something eternal and complete that it is within her power to reveal. Plato's idea of reminiscence, or anamnesis, works in a similar way to suggest that the past was always there, an immanent presence that is contrasted with sense perception, which reveals only glimpses of the true.[40]

Just as the self-consciousness of Odysseus had thrust him into history – as a self-determining subject – and created the past as something both distant and essential to his very being, so modernity's recognition of itself as a distinct epoch, Blumenberg wrote, 'simultaneously created the other epochs'.[41] These epochs subsequently become the far-flung domains of potential knowledge that might reveal how the past became separated from the present, and perhaps also an awareness of what was lost, as in the case, for instance, of the 'historiographical recovery of the Middle Ages', a time that had until then not been the subject of any great interest but which, from a modern perspective, is 'constructed' as an epoch in terms of its legacy to the modern period. This inheritance was hitherto suppressed, Blumenberg suggests, but is now admitted in the new, self-conscious present.[42] Some of the early modern historical prospectors of the Western heritage were keen to see fact take precedence over fiction and fancy. For Edward Gibbon, inspired by his encounter with the ruined remains of Rome to write *The History of the Decline and Fall of the Roman Empire* (1766–88), the historical endeavour was not ostensibly one of recreating or 'remembering' the past: it was, according to one philosopher of history, taken with a particular idea of 'past history as the play of irrational forces'.[43] In addition to which there was the problem of the authenticity of events that were distant from experience and beyond the realms of any living memory. 'The past was littered with frauds and forgeries, with hagiography and romance', Joseph Levine says, 'and it was the first duty of the historian . . . to root out the fictions that disturbed it.'[44]

In other terms, this was an aspect of the 'historical sublime', 'a liminal phenomenon demarcating the phase of the subjective mind from the objective mind'.[45] This past, which proved elusive and far from any attempts to reconcile it with contemporary knowledge or 'to impose meaning', had all the same occupied the thoughts and efforts of historians until the nineteenth century.[46] What replaced it reflected the prevailing empiricism of the day, in which the key to historical accuracy – or the truth, *alethia* (the ancient Greek 'unforgetting') – was to be found in evidence. The crossing of the liminal threshold that takes us out of the historical sublime, Frank Ankersmit remarks, makes history

> an almost tangible reality . . . One really feels that from now on one belongs to a different world and that a former part of ourselves has died off and become a lifeless and empty shell.[47]

'The disciplinization of historical writing' meant that the past began to lose its sense of strangeness; it 'became more common, more domesticated, more a variant of an eternal present'.[48] Knowledge of antiquity, for instance, saw to it that in psychological and philosophical terms at least, our historical antecedents were often seen to extend far beyond any recognizable homeland of the kind that nostalgia seeks. 'The true ancestors of the European nations', John Stuart Mill wrote,

> are not those from whose blood they sprang . . . but those from whom they derive the richest portion of their inheritance. The battle of Marathon, even as an event in English history, is of more importance than the battle of Hastings.[49]

But it was the question of precisely what historical knowledge consisted in that can reveal something of the ways in which the idea of memory as it relates to history, and to the past, developed in the last two centuries.[50] In general terms, when we speak of memory, we are often referring to something more than memory in the sense of, say, recollection or remembering. Perhaps this is a 'something' that acts as a prompt – a smell, a document, a place and so on. But such examples demonstrate not only the slipperiness of the term 'memory' but the fact that it is attached to other things; one of which, of course, is historical thought. Pierre Nora, one of the key figures in the burgeoning trans-disciplinary field of memory studies, for instance, claimed that history is indeed not the same thing as memory, but that it nonetheless forms one part of a host of contemporary *lieux de mémoire* (*realms* or *spaces* of memory) found in contemporary society, and which now seem to form our main connection to tradition, and to a past that once might have been constituted through living, organic and communal relations (or, in other words, 'collective memory').[51] Paul Ricoeur, too, insists on an 'epistemological break' separating memory and history, evident in the clear difference between collective memory and history (which is impersonal, or at least non-intimate), which can be seen, for instance, in the contrasting kinds of knowledge inherent in 'told stories' on the one hand and 'history built on documentary traces' on the other.[52]

But it is precisely because self-consciousness creates a split in the world (an idea we keep coming back to), breaking apart the rhythms of tradition and tearing the fabric of immemorial time, that history at the most general level gets taken for memory. Oral traditions, and the collective sense of belonging that is fixed to language and culture, for instance, are largely swept aside in modern societies. Where they persist, it is against the tides of change, and as echoes of a past that risks being overwhelmed by the force of time's relentless forward thrust. As Berman noted, the existential split exemplified in the break with tradition produced an 'inner dichotomy' – especially among inhabitants of nineteenth-century cities, who were able to remember what it was 'like to live, materially and spiritually, in worlds that are [were] not modern at all'. It gave rise in modernity, more generally, to a 'sense of living in two worlds simultaneously'.[53]

In the West we may have become more accustomed to the constant upheaval, which is so normal as to be unexceptional, but those living in fast-changing, 'modernizing' societies the world over are today undergoing the same kind of separation from the past, which will likely result in a similar feeling of loss. The experience of the modern world thus gives us the idea that there is a past from which we have become alienated. Yet should it or could it be recovered, we suspect that this past would be the very thing that was lost, the 'memory' of the vanished world that might restore us to a kind of unity, a sense of belonging and being at home.

Leaving aside some of the more complicated aspects of the epistemological break between memory and history for the time being, it is nonetheless the case that historical knowledge was – particularly in the early efforts of important figures in the formation of modernity – indisputably, and without apparent complication, located within the realm of memory. This association was due in particular to the influence of Francis Bacon, whose *Instauratio magna* (1620) was at the forefront of work that sought to set knowledge on a more scientific basis. Bacon's importance to the Enlightenment was crucial and widely recognized in Britain and France, particularly his 'mapping of knowledge via the three fundamental faculties of mind – memory, reason and imagination', which saw him 'adopted as the Royal Society's mascot'.[54] In this formulation memory becomes the realm of one specific area of knowledge, history, while reason and imagination were the realms of philosophy and poetry respectively.

The hold of the Baconian view of memory and history began to loosen with the rise of historicism (the professionalization of history as a discipline) in the nineteenth century, but it still held enough sway that it could be the target of attack for one of the leading philosophers of history some 400 years after it was first assumed. In *The Idea of History*, a series of writings from the 1930s published posthumously in 1946, R. G. Collingwood, then Waynflete Professor of Metaphysical Philosophy at Oxford, set out to debunk what he referred to as the 'common-sense theory about history', derived from Bacon, that 'the essential things in history are memory and authority':

If an event or state of things is to be historically known, first of all someone must be acquainted with it; then he must remember it; then he must state his recollection of it in terms intelligible to another; and finally that other must accept the statement as true.[55]

History in the Baconian sense could then be boiled down to 'believing someone else when he says that he remembers something'.[56] While Collingwood accepted that the two Baconian constituents in this understanding of history had assumed such importance due to their improvement on older, medieval approaches to the study of the past – often badly conceived, error-strewn or, indeed, still holding on to tales of legends that had no factual basis – they could not lead to an accurate or truthful view of the past, especially when so much of the past is mediated through materials that are not direct testimonies. 'Bacon's definition of history as the realm of memory was wrong', Collingwood wrote, 'because the past only requires historical investigation so far as it is not and cannot be remembered.'[57]

The challenge for the idea of historical truth, for Collingwood, was inseparable from evidence – documents, data and so on – and perspective, both of which took the historian away from the idea of the past being within grasp of living memory. The realm of history was thus the unremembered. It was necessary to keep in mind that this meant history was concerned with the mutual relationship between, on the one hand, the past itself, and on the other, what the historian thought *into* that past; about the events of the past and the act of inquiring into them, and so on.[58] On the side of the temporal divide occupied by the historian, it can be said to be a matter of looking, seeing and reimagining, or even rethinking, the past. Seeing, witnessing and picturing, as Jacques Le Goff points out, are bound up in the origins of the word 'history'.[59] Unsurprisingly, then, history has sought to make the past available or transparent in a way that has encouraged the use of picture metaphors: the capturing of life, its realization. This is evident, Ankersmit writes, in the exhortation that a reader 'look through' the writing of history much as a viewer would look through naturalist paintings to find some corresponding (but absent) reality that represented truth or accuracy.[60]

For Collingwood, it seemed that the historian was the conduit for this vision of the past, making something akin to an empathetic leap from the present perspective into the mind of the past. The historian, in other words, only understands the past when it appears to him as if it were his present. 'When a man thinks historically', Collingwood wrote, 'he has before him certain documents or relics of the past':

> His business is to discover what the past was which left these relics behind it. For example, the relics are certain written words; and in that case he has to discover what the person who wrote those words meant by them. This means discovering the thought which he expressed by them. To discover what this thought was, the historian must think it again for himself.[61]

Whether or not Collingwood was as careful as he might have been in the outline of such a procedure, to think something again is very much like trying to repeat or recollect: to make available to public memory 'the unremembered'. Such a notion of how the past can be known, encountered and, indeed, remembered at such a distance of time and experience was subject to sceptical doubts that verged on derision. 'Collingwood', E. H. Carr suggests in *What Is History?*, 'comes perilously near to treating history as something spun out of the human brain.'[62] Arthur C. Danto equally spotted a 'repertoire of methodologically dubious aids':

> Empathic intuitions, sympathetic understandings, vicarious identifications and the like through the exploitation of which the mind of the historian was to achieve harmonic resonance with other minds in other areas, across the otherwise impenetrable insulations of time and change.[63]

Thus the principal charge against Collingwood was that such reimaginings obliterated the possibility of objective knowledge of the past; yet, on the other hand, to look at the progress of historiography – at the history of history – is surely to see, as Le Goff writes, only the complications of a notion such as objectivity. Instead what seems to be clearer, more characteristic, even, is the centrality of the one who does the looking and who produces, as a result, 'a series of new readings of the past, full of losses and resurgences, of memory gaps and revisions'.[64]

As 'processes of insight', David Lowenthal argues, memory and history share much, and the 'shadowy boundaries' that separate them can often be difficult to discern.[65] Even the sense that history, relying on evidence that can be challenged, does not share memory's apparent quality of immediate certainty does not get over the difficulties raised by the apparent autonomy of the historian's gaze.

Changes in the scale of perspective – the attempt to zoom in or out of some part of the past – produce yet more philosophical problems for obtaining reliable or meaningful knowledge of the past. If Collingwood's subjectivist approach mingled history with recollection – history, he implied, engages the unremembered – it was perhaps one early statement of a postmodern turn in the ideas of how the past might be recovered, which may therefore relate it to Pierre Nora's elaboration of the *lieux de mémoire*.[66] Yet one thinker and historian, who, Simon Schama notes, 'has written most imaginatively, courageously, and rigorously on the opportunities and perils of tracking the evidence of social memory', the Italian 'microhistorian' Carlo Ginzburg, has attempted to engage the traces of the past as itself a kind of 'unconscious', with all the Freudian connotations that term gives rise to. It is an approach that contrasts starkly with more dominant 'macro' approaches to history, where intention and agency are far more important in giving an account of history's unfolding.[67]

Aside from the distance between the historian and the object of interest, Ginzburg's approach – known as 'microhistory' – might in some ways be said to produce a picture of the past that is rather less like a realist painting and rather more like the kind of documentary films with which we are now so familiar, and which attempt to offer up a slice of real life from some apparently insignificant corner of existence, all the while producing revelations that have much broader ramifications. More pertinent in terms of this discussion is Ginzburg's appeal to Leibniz's 'Monadology' as a means of thinking through the nature of the historical perspective. Leibniz's theory of the monad, in short, permits 'the development of a model of cognition based on a plurality of points of view', which are 'little worlds' in Leibniz's language, and which taken together make up an immanent whole.[68] In other words, it is a method that aims for a level of *visual* detail and a sense of presence that might pitch a reader back into a vividly realized past, almost as if the image or object it produces is an unvarnished piece of that distant reality suddenly washed up on our shores. In looking for the 'infinitesimal traces' that could 'permit the comprehension of a deeper, otherwise unattainable reality', Ginzburg saw that the challenge was to engage a folk memory of habits and practices that did not necessarily exist at the level of abstract knowledge characteristic of modern written culture. Rather, in the absence of documentation, they might only be evident as dim and distant echoes of the past.[69] One question, then, was how to approach a past where knowledge was not only not documented in written form, but which would also often have been reflexive, automatic or unconscious – and no less important for any attempt to recall or 'picture' the past. For instance:

> The ability to identify a defective horse by the condition of his hocks, an impending storm by sudden changes in the wind, a hostile intention in a sudden change of expression, was certainly not to be learned from a farmer's manual or meteorological or psychological treatises. Knowledge of this sort, in each instance, was richer than any written codification.[70]

The depth of such a 'local' knowledge rooted in the everyday, but which can easily vanish under the lens of abstraction (with its summarizing, codifying and generalizing), suggests, of course, the particularity of actual lived time and the existence of micro-worlds. To the extent that they embodied immemorial habit, these monadic, self-contained worlds would be 'without origin, memory, or history'.[71] The past that, for Ginzburg, could not be represented without losing something deeper or more essential, takes on – in Frank Ankersmit's words – 'a reality that had previously only been attributed to the past', now reconstructed as a fragment that might reflect more universal truths.[72] A key part of Ginzburg's defence of his work is that history, in its reconstruction of the past, had been too reliant on an 'aristocratic conception of culture' that could only see in the lives of the mostly illiterate, uneducated lower classes a degraded or distorted picture of a given period of time.[73] This had been the reason all that was known hitherto about such people were inferences made from written sources attached to a dominant culture that might easily, and probably did, distort the 'thoughts, beliefs, and . . . aspirations' of 'peasants and artisans'.[74] The key idea, then, was to find a way of showing how a unique and repressed culture might reveal itself.

In Ginzburg's *The Cheese and the Worms* an attempt was made to recover such a 'half obliterated' fragment of a reality. It was made accessible through the trial records and testimonies of a sixteenth-century miller named Menocchio, who had been tried as a heretic for repeatedly asserting a set of beliefs that amounted to the blasphemous view that 'the world had its origin in putrefaction'.[75] It was the discovery of a brief description of the trial record that engaged Ginzburg's interest in the events surrounding Menocchio. He suspected that this heretical view might be the way into a much deeper understanding of the 'popular culture' of a past that had long since vanished. Yet without the wider understanding of the heresies as phenomena belonging to a culture that had not been recorded or preserved, and was at this point wholly forgotten, all that remained were the trial records. Menocchio's own account of his unique world view, as recorded in the records of the Holy Office of the Inquisition, gives an indication of the puzzle that faced Ginzburg. Before the Creation, Menocchio had told the trial, 'all was chaos':

> that is, earth, air, water, and fire were mixed together; and out of that bulk a mass formed – just as cheese is made out of milk – and worms appeared in it, and these were the angels. The most holy majesty decreed that these should be God and the angels . . . created out of that mass at the same time.[76]

These testimonies baffled the authorities and concerned most of Menocchio's contemporaries, but by adding a host of other documents that showed the miller's 'readings and discussions, his thoughts and his sentiments – fears, hopes, ironies, rages, despairs', Ginzburg felt it was possible 'to bring him very close to us', thus revealing 'a man like ourselves: one of us'.[77]

This, though, was a kind of history that was 'intended to be a story as well as a piece of writing'.[78] It was a history that was not, Ankersmit charged, representative of anything but itself.[79] '"Reality" has invaded representation' to produce a rather different kind of history:

> What remains are these 'chunks of the past', these raw stories about apparently quite irrelevant historical occurrences that leave most contemporary historians just as baffled as the visitors to the museum of sixty years ago when they were confronted with Duchamp's ready-mades.[80]

Ankersmit here raises an interesting comparison that leads us into a further aspect of the monadic fragment as it is found in microhistory: namely the unconscious as a kind of involuntary memory of something hitherto concealed. Marcel Duchamp's readymades, we might recall, did not emerge from any conventional attempt at artistic self-expression. They were 'found' objects, usually of little or no worth (a bottle rack, a urinal, a snow shovel), but somehow turned into art by the declaration – even whim – of the artist; by a manoeuvre that took them from one context (the functional, utilitarian world, for instance) and placed them in an entirely different one (the aesthetic world of the museum). There is something in what Ankersmit says as it relates to how we expect details, fragments or phenomena that are raised to our level of awareness to represent or reflect knowledge of a world that has already been substantially enriched by its prior existents; that is to say, to be representative also of a method employed by a historian that proceeds from a background of what is known and what further points of interest emerge as gaps in knowledge from this. Ginzburg, though, works from the point of view of the anomalous and the enigmatic; as he himself says, like a detective looking for clues. Thus he accidentally stumbled upon the case of Menocchio without any prior sense that he would encounter such a tale. The status of the miller's story, additionally, adds to the controversial nature of such a historical procedure because it seems to be a one-off, making Menocchio 'unrepresentative', 'irrelevant' and so on – unless, of course, we take Ginzburg's approach to be essentially Leibnizian, and therefore convinced that particularity reflects universality.

Although implicitly sceptical of the implications of microhistory, what is equally noteworthy about Ankersmit's analogy of the ready-made is that Ginzburg would likely not disagree that he was engaging, as did the readymades, unconscious elements of a reality that seemed to come out of nowhere.[81] But the basis of the shock that microhistory delivered, such as it was to other historians, is a result of the fact that a more macro-historical view would not bother looking at something so apparently worthless. In this instance, Menocchio's case reveals a past which has not been, or cannot be, represented. Thus access to it proceeds much in the way Freud did when he sought in 'details of little importance . . . even trivial or minor' – slips of the tongue, neurotic tics – the route to some higher truth about the self.[82]

Microhistory, Paul Ricoeur says in his discussion of Ginzburg, cannot be the 'resurrection of the lived experience of social agents', or a route back into some lost 'collective memory', because the past it reconstitutes is always based on social interactions that are documented and constructed from an array of sources.[83] What Ginzburg's microhistory seems nonetheless to present is a variant on Collingwood's 'unremembered' past, but done in such a way that casts it as the unconscious trace, or reflection of, a macro-history – a history, let's say, of the dominant narrative that obscures a 'culture of the people' – much like Leibniz's monads, 'which, nevertheless, are nothing but aspects [perspectives] of a single universe, according to the special point of view of each monad'.[84]

In other words, whether it is history or story, we might see the past in Ginzburg as something like a recovered memory, resulting from a new effort to penetrate deeper within a particular picture of the past, as one might do with a photographic enlargement. There is a 'reciprocal relationship between macro- and microhistory', Ginzburg notes, 'between wide shots and close-ups'.[85] The latter reveal the implications of a seeing that produces an image of the past which, like Walter Benjamin's notion of an 'optical unconscious' – as if a camera was autonomously doing the seeing that escaped normal, unaided human perception – penetrates a reality whose outward appearance may offer deceptive truths to our understanding of the past.[86]

40-48

Heritage and the Surfeit of Memory

The appearance of the past as a possible object of experience might be said to identify history as an endeavour that would take up a role in shaping public memory in a peculiarly modern way – one that perhaps distances and orders it; keeps it in its place. But when we look back now at the remark of a sceptical Nietzsche, in his *Untimely Meditations*, who saw himself living in a time when 'memory opens all its gates' to the past – to 'strange guests' that flow in 'unceasingly from inexhaustible wells' – we might be forgiven for taking him as our direct contemporary, reporting on a world in which the distinction of past from present becomes ever more difficult to maintain.[87] From architecture that pastiches eighteenth-century styles to anniversary celebrations of almost anything that has been deemed at some point to be culturally significant, it seems that we are no longer as convinced of the need to forget as Nietzsche was. The truth is that remnants of the past, which make up the sphere of cultural memory, have become part of the furniture of our everyday life, and in ways that are becoming so commonplace that little notice is taken of the fact.

In recent years one of the oddest examples of the appearance of these strange guests of yesteryear has been the BBC Parliament television channel's practice of rebroadcasting an entire UK General Election Day coverage from some bygone year (it typically happens while Parliament itself is in recess, and there are no contemporary events meriting media coverage). We might usefully compare this phenomenon to the normal coverage of political history on television. These returns to bygone years are not simply casting a glance back at significant events of the past, which is something that is much more commonplace in television programming and usually peppered with the views of contemporary historians and commentators. Their presence always keeps us – the viewers – more or less anchored in the here and now, and they remind us that we are looking at all this from the perspective of today, and perhaps because there are lessons of some kind to be learned from revisiting some era, or some historical event. By contrast, the General Election repeats are more a kind of virtual reality in which the broadcast, running for an entire day, is exactly in sync with the viewer's time of day, allowing one to be almost sucked into this other time and space. When I glanced at my clock and saw that it was 10.30 a.m., and the date was 5 May, it was a fact that seemed to be confirmed by turning back to the broadcast, which revealed that it was indeed, 10.30 a.m. on that very date. The only difference, of course, was that in the television reality – which is to say, the virtual reality – it was 1970 and not 2011.

This invitation to be pulled back into the past, David Lowenthal suggested, is not necessarily anything new. Other times and places can, of course, be conjured up by a mind turned inwards through any number of causes – 'drugs, dreams, knocks in the head, pacts with the devil, lightning bolts, thunder claps, and since H. G. Wells, time machines'.[88] Lowenthal was writing in the 1980s, so he had yet to see the inherent possibilities of multi-channel TV (let alone the Internet), whose many portals may indeed appear to deliver something of the impact of a time machine. Journeying back to 1970 via the BBC Parliament channel's time machine, I was able to marvel – as an anthropologist might do on first arriving in some strange land – at how different its inhabitants were to those of 2011; the fact that politicians and pundits seemed to be all men, and that these men seemed to unthinkingly light up cigarettes (or pipes) as they heatedly discussed the balance of power in the nation.

There is, though, an abundance of detail to be glimpsed in achieving such a 'real-time' connection to a past brought back to life (which is yet always unrecoverable) in the kind of details that charge memory into action like a Proustian madeleine. How slow and unfussed that world seemed. Those 'strange guests', as Nietzsche might have seen them, were sometimes younger incarnations of well-known figures who still roam the TV network today, then unwitting pioneers in what we now call rolling broadcast news. It was not the simple passage of the four decades that located them in their time and place, but the actual sense of lost time one obtained from such 'real-time', at-a-distance viewing. It was all there in the details of a world that would have been taken for granted but which – from the perspective of the multi-channel TV surfer of today – seemed so archaic. It could be glimpsed in the frequent recourse of the presenter – the late Robin Day, then operating without earpiece or autocue – to a large GPO telephone that sat on his desk, from which he would receive messages from the programme director or reports from correspondents in far-flung corners of the country such as the Outer Hebrides. This was the past as a present now gone; one that will always be locked inside its analogue media landscape, itself now released through the capacious vistas of digital memory, if only as a recollection of how we used to be.

Nietzsche wrote the second of his *Untimely Meditations* on the 'utility and liability of history for life' – advocating the importance of forgetting the past – long before the contemporary memory boom, which would seem to have made his remarks more apposite. The effects of this memory boom have to be seen as a peculiarly post-modern variant of understanding or grappling with the past. The surfeit of recollection (Nietzsche writes of a 'surfeit of history') made available by the media, and by a 'cultural sector' whose chief com-modity is the past, ensures that the world we inhabit is overcome with reminders of past events, memorials to the departed and recre-ations of how we used to live. For Nietzsche, memory was 'a primal determinant of human being', but one that was too easily lured into an obliviousness to present concerns.[89] When we look at the triumph of heritage culture, there is a sense that his words ring true today. His disregard for history and historians had a particular target, how-ever: 'antiquarians' whose 'memory revolves unwearyingly in a circle', forever more interested in the past than in the present.[90] History in other forms – 'monumental' and 'critical' – would be of useful service to life, he thought, because they were not fixed solely on the past. Nietzsche's dislike for the first kind of historical endeavour was not unusual, as Rosemary Sweet suggests in a recent study of antiquaries. The antiquary was a kind of under-labourer for the greater critical endeavour, and thus

> history occupied a place of much higher regard . . . in the same way that art in the classical style occupied a place of infinitely greater esteem than did the depiction of everyday life, with its minute realisation of quotidian details.[91]

The problem for Nietzsche, one that again might ring true to contemporary experience, was the lack of discrimination: 'Everything old and past that enters one's field of vision at all is in the end blandly taken to be worthy of reverence.'[92] What is recognizable in Nietzsche's view of an obsession with the past that seems to originate in a desire for any old rubbish, just as long as it is old, is the urge to preserve 'the past' in almost any form it takes. Early modern antiquaries with a fascination for dead stuff – rare books, souvenirs, antiques – had always been interested in preserving something that appeared as the relic of a more interesting past.

Equally, Schama has shown, the modern world threw up, in its romantics and nature-lovers, people who were always ineluctably drawn to preserving what they saw of nature around them – if it happened to protrude through 'the commonplaces of contemporary life', that is.[93] The memory of landscape is the past understood in a non-historiographical sense, but one that accords with today's heritage culture. It is the eco-home recovered in some sense through the restoration or preservation of ruins, or in the establishment of memorial gardens and national parks, but as spaces of a kind of common national memory. So, while such leaps into the past are not particularly new – they may have a new focus or object of interest – the tendency picks up momentum in contemporary society, as 'heritage' locates ever more objects of interest. In Britain, our contemporary understanding of heritage – as, roughly, the preservation of 'cultures', both local and national, natural and human-made, existing in things and in ways of speaking and doing – would seem to date from around the 1940s. It represents a tendency that has benefited from a 'vast inflation', its chief chronicler Raphael Samuel argued, 'being extended to environments and artefacts which in the past would have been regarded as falling beneath the dignity of history'.[94] From Roman ruins and old battlefields to 'shrinking wetlands' and 'roadside verges' (home to many species of plant and animal that are 'our heritage'), it is a phenomenon of wildly heterogeneous 'theatres' of memory that stage contemporary culture's fixation on the past as a kind of memory of who we really are.[95]

This idea of the past was found, most clearly, in the kind of sentiments that identified a sense of belonging with a mythopoeic imaginary:

It was in the Second World War – the 'People's War' as it was proclaimed, at the time when enemy invasion seemed imminent – that a radical, patriotic version of the idea of heritage seemed to enter into its own ... it informed, indeed inspired, the wartime films of Humphrey Jennings, as for example in Words of Battle, where RAF pilots are pictured assembling round a Spitfire while, in a voice-over, Milton's *Areopagitica* describes a 'mighty and puissant nation' shaking her locks ... The neo-romantic, Communist-leaning *Our Time* ... ran a regular 'Heritage' feature, using a suitably Gothic font and culling passages from Chaucer, Shakespeare and Wordsworth.[96]

For Raphael Samuel, an advocate of 'bottom-up' history who established the History Workshop in the 1970s to explore the possibilities of what we now term 'social memory' studies, culture's move into a space of heritage was apparently without limit. 'Lexically', he wrote, heritage was a term 'capacious enough to accommodate wildly discrepant meanings'.[97] Thus we see that it refers not merely to royal palaces and great country houses but to railway sidings, canalside walks, industrial warehouses remade as luxury flats, wasteland wildlife sanctuaries, folk song, urban conservation movements and so on.

Like the sense of the past that appeared to indicate some kind of crisis for those who first realized they were living in a new and modern epoch – one determinedly set apart from the Middle Ages and antiquity – the rise of heritage can be a matter of concern: an indication more of what has been lost in the re-presentation of the past than of the richness of the presumed cultural history it makes available. Pierre Nora, who coined the term *les lieux de mémoire* to describe the 'sites of memory' that, like the world of heritage described by Samuel, encapsulate or illustrate some of the causes and effects of this postmodern remaking of memory through a kind of 'history' (rather than as something embodied in lived habit), dated the appearance of the phenomenon in his native France to the 1930s.[98] 'The moment of *lieux de mémoire* occurs at the same time that an immense and intimate fund of memory disappears', which is to say, with the eclipse of tradition and waning of nationalistic sentiment. What remains, he argues, is just that: *remains*, things, remnants, parts of a whole that in their isolation from habit and tradition stand ultimately for 'the deritualization' of the world. Thus *lieux de mémoire*, which he takes to include 'museums, archives, cemeteries, festivals, anniversaries', originate with

> the sense that there is no spontaneous memory, that we must deliberately create archives, maintain anniversaries, organize celebrations, pronounce eulogies, and notarize bills because such activities no longer occur naturally.[99]

Over the length and breadth of the UK and other countries, in many a town or city – and this may apply in almost any post-industrial nation – the demise of the economic forces, infrastructures and ways of life and work that first produced the impetus towards modern urban life, beginning in earnest around the 1960s, has been followed by the slow rise of the phenomenon of heritage and the prospect of the riches promised by the tourism that goes along with the reanimation of recently moribund industrial topographies, now established as a kind of open-air museum of modernity's past. Thus the heritage

A D-Day re-enactment in 2002, on the anniversary of the Normandy landings of 6 June 1944. Pictured here are two historical stand-ins gazing at an information display as they try to fathom a past they did not live.

and museum spaces that often now occupy sites of industrial ruins – or 'excessive space', according to the geographer Tim Edensor – 'seamlessly banish ambiguity and the multiplicity of the past' and aim instead for something that is capable of being assimilated within the culture of leisure and consumption.[100]

'Slowly, bit by bit', Christine Boyer reminds us, 'forgotten waterfronts, underutilized manufacturing areas, down-trodden inner-city neighbourhoods' became revalued for their intrinsic 'pastness':

> the parts of the city that modern architects and planners had neglected or simply overlooked, were placed behind regulatory boundaries, their architectural patrimony entrusted to protection societies and their aesthetic appearances constantly rehabilitated and revitalized.[101]

These new heritage zones represent, David Lowenthal writes, the 'spoils of history'.[102] But how could heritage, the promise of a return to the past, be anything other than unfaithful to the real past? Is it any more likely to distort than reveal, to display its best baubles and leave aside the carbuncles – and the bone-grinding drudgery that was the reality of this quaint, museum-style ghost of a past?

The contemporary city's 'history' is in keeping with Nora's conflation of history and memory as the principal pathology of 'post-' societies: post-industrial, postcolonial and more generally postmodern. There is perhaps no way of ever recovering what is gone in terms of the kind of 'spontaneous memory' whose demise Nora laments, but we can perhaps fill in the background, the scenery, to imaginatively conjure up the place that these 'strange guests' belonged to.

In W. G. Sebald's *The Emigrants*, a work of prose fiction with strong autobiographical elements, we are able to contextualize an actual present within layers of memory. As the narrator recounts his arrival in Manchester from Germany in the mid-1960s (Sebald himself moved there in 1966), he describes many journeys taken on foot through increasingly post-industrial landscapes that were then still littered with historical remnants – mill houses abandoned, chimney stacks that once belched dust and smoke into the atmosphere, disused canals – that would have been a common sight in Friedrich Engels's

The cover of an
English Heritage
brochure (2008).

ENGLISH HERITAGE

Ordinary Landscapes, Special Places

Anfield, Breckfield and the growth
of Liverpool's suburbs

days as a Manchester mill owner in the 1840s.[103] The reader who
approaches this work today with a knowledge of the city's contemporary transformations might then glimpse the past at several levels:
first, from the reader's present perspective; second, from the narrator's
present perspective, which is to say 1966; and third, the city in 1945
as seen through the memory of Max Ferber, a central figure in the
book, whose acquaintance gives the narrator spiritual sustenance in
this strange place. We learn that Ferber arrived in Manchester after
the Second World War, an immigrant, like the narrator, and occupied
a studio in an abandoned industrial area of the city.

The ghost of the past in the present – and, we can read here, heritage culture's obsession with the past – becomes apparent through
an awareness that many of these Manchester canals and mill buildings
that lay abandoned in the 1966 of Sebald's narrator have today been
refurbished and now form a large part of the city's commercial appeal
in terms of urban regeneration (apartments for young professionals,
offices for businesses) and tourism. But the real – and vanished –
nature of that past, though glimpsed as a trace in photographs or
old film reels, can perhaps only be encountered in the recollection
of one, like Sebald's Ferber, who feels its absence as a loss. Arriving
in the city on foot, and having walked many miles across the

countryside from Yorkshire to get there, Ferber first catches sight of Manchester in panorama, the whole of it lit by the glow of the industrial topography, 'as if by firelight or Bengal flares':

> Not until this illumination died (said Ferber) did his eye roam, taking in the crammed and interlinked rows of houses, the textile mills and dying works, the gasometers, chemicals plants and factories of every kind, as far as what he took to be the centre of the city, where all seemed one solid mass of utter blackness, bereft of any further distinguishing features. The most impressive thing, of course, said Ferber, were all the chimneys that towered above the plain and flat maze of housing, as far as the eye could see . . . thousands of them, side by side, belching out smoke day and night.[104]

To occupy the reader's present is to be conscious of how much of this has gone at the same time as parts of it are revived as urban museum; it is to be aware of the intervention of time, and the removal of traces, and how these together bring the erasure of continuous memory of place. In most post-industrial societies, what was sandwiched between the real past, and this present that consists of spaces adorned with carefully tended and preserved representations of the past, was the future. That future, associated with modernism, was all about applying the Nietzschean remedy: an 'active forgetfulness' that was 'like a doorkeeper' holding the past at bay to preserve a sense of sanity amid the surfeit of history and memory.[105]

The Infinitesimal

In August 1969, I ran away; and, preoccupied as I have been in developing these thoughts on memory, the event has become something that has nagged away at the reliability of my own earliest recollections. To the extent that I may say that I remember, it is remembrance of small details, which on their own are not necessarily a source of accurate knowledge about the past. But any of us confronted with the role of memory in the making of self are likely to be drawn quite naturally to reflecting on our own pasts; on people, places and events that have, in important and perhaps enigmatic ways, informed the selves that we have become, and continue becoming.

There are those aspects of any past that may be unwelcome, yet stubbornly resist our attempts to obliterate them. We often talk of our earliest memories, very personal memories that perhaps return us to a time when we were very young. Running away on my first day at school, after being apparently deposited at the school gates by my mother, may be my earliest memory, but it exerts less of a pull on me than another event that took place some months later, although it is only now that I know this. Hearing George Harrison's recording of 'My Sweet Lord' on several discrete occasions recently has been enough to bring it back to me and to plunge me back into a past that seemed to have been long gone, erased by the forward momentum of time and the accumulation of more recent experience. As I hear this song in the present I feel curiously within reach of the past, and the school gymnasium where on one particular day I, along with the other boys, was cajoled into politely approaching our female classmates to ask for a dance. 'My Sweet Lord', a song that invokes the sacred in its use of mantras, was itself played repeatedly on the turntable as we were instructed in the social niceties of asking a member of the opposite sex to dance, the song all the while writing its way into me.

Much, however, remains vague. The sense of that time – or, more accurately, the fleeting appearance of piecemeal mental images (triangular milk cartons with straws, sitting attentively in class listening to a broadcast of Homer's *Iliad*, a favourite pair of shoes adorned with buckles, the smell and feel of plasticine, which came in strips of four or five 'tubes' that could be torn off), all accompanied by often intense feelings and a sense that a moment so distant might actually be within grasp – returns with such force that I wonder now what else might relate to that day that could allow me to comprehend the impression it has left on me.

Perhaps it presents itself as the shadow of some primordial unity of experience that could be best described as a kind of 'home'; not just in the sense of lost tradition and community, or of nostalgia for an earlier and more simple way of life. Rather, I think these experiences take shape unwittingly until we end up carrying them around; it is the ultimately fruitless search for the child you were and the possibilities that have now been played out or are gone forever, as the case may be. This is one more consequence of a self-consciousness of a separation of oneself from the world, and from others, which did not bother you as a child because you were always 'at home'. The child who enters self-consciousness arrives, Peter Sloterdijk remarks, in a 'divided world'.[106] In his recent attempt to think of the human at home as being located in a multiplicity of 'spheres' – 'the interior, disclosed, shared realm, inhabited by humans' – he notes that we are thrust into an existence that resides in 'an outside', but which carries 'inner worlds':

> It's too late to dream ourselves back to a place under celestial domes whose interiors would permit domestic feelings of order. That security in the largest circle has been destroyed for those in the know, along with the old homely, immunizing cosmos itself.[107]

Getting back to that place would be to rewind experience and undo knowledge and self-consciousness. You had no memory then, as a child; you were just there in the time and place you were, and that was it. But, as the years pass, that seemingly changes into an awareness of an immutable connection that is intensified by the knowledge that you can't go back. Not only that: when it comes down to it, you have barely any recollection of what you want, or feel compelled, to recover. Hence the sense that memory – especially the sense of being overcome by a feeling that is unwilled, which Proust termed involuntary memory – is, like death, inescapable.

*

IF IT WAS NO COINCIDENCE that the formal properties of a song make it something that would easily lodge itself in an impressionable young mind at such a symbolic moment in early life, it seems equally to be an odd coincidence that George Harrison's hymn-like song was itself at least partly born of an unconscious act of remembrance, specifically, of another song – 'He's So Fine' by The Chiffons – which Harrison was later accused of plagiarizing in a well-known court case. But for millennia the song as a form has been one means of remembering that flourished within human communities. Words put together with melodies can be easily learned, which is to say, memorized. But in the era of mediated popular culture of the last 100 years or so the song would become a record, an object that was produced to engage the repetition of play. Thus recorded songs, as Friedrich Kittler has written, catch up with us, 'killing us softly' in their power to undo and remake a present moment as they take us somewhere else.[108] They represent one example of the power of the infinitesimal to shape the present. Walter Benjamin, who as we have already noted was convinced of the 'hieroglyphic' nature of modern material culture, which was thus capable of revealing a greater truth than simple things or objects of everyday life might suggest, could see no end of memory:

> He who has once begun to open the fan of memory never comes to the end of its segments. No image satisfies him, for he has seen that it can be unfolded, and only in its folds does the truth reside – that image, that taste, that touch for whose sake all this has been unfurled and dissected; and now remembrance progresses from small to smallest details, from the smallest to the infinitesimal, while that which it encounters in these microcosms grows ever mightier.[109]

Memory for Benjamin thus revolves around small things – toys, names, images that appear distant to consciousness. 'I have once more entered a period of small writing', he wrote in a letter in 1926: 'even after long intervals, I always find some kind of home again'.[110] Recollection, for Benjamin, is akin to the now increasingly obsolete process of producing photographic blow-ups from tiny film negatives to hone in on the details of everyday life that children characteristically see, and that adults – living always multi-temporally – are typically oblivious to. It seems apt that a key section in *One-way Street*, one of his pivotal works touching on childhood and memory, is titled 'Enlargements', because the effect of zooming in has the visual, optical impact of penetrating a surface image to reveal ever more depth.

'Enlargements' sees Benjamin turn his thoughts to moments from childhood, which are then illuminated just enough to allow a sudden apprehension to reach the crucial tiny detail, the miniscule clue, which then becomes central to how we perceive the larger 'image'. The aim is to reverse the irretrievability of the past. Recollection thus creates a world within a world, like that which we find in Benjamin's image or evocation of a carousel in the autobiographical text *A Berlin Childhood Around 1900*, which seems to hold out the possibility of retrieval in such inward voyaging:

> The revolving deck with its obliging animals skims the surface of the ground. It is at the height best suited to dreams of flying. Music rings out – and with a jolt, the child rolls away from his mother. At first, he is afraid to leave her. But then he notices how he himself is faithful. He is enthroned, as faithful monarch, above a world that belongs to him. Trees and natives line the borders at intervals. Suddenly his mother reappears in an Orient. Then, from some primeval forest, comes a treetop – one such as the child has seen already thousands of years ago, such as he has seen just now, for the first time, on a carousel.[111]

Objects of all kinds, brought into view through the work of recollection, are made to reveal their hieroglyphic potential to open the imagination to reflections not only of a world outside, but of a world that – from the child's point of view – was draped in mystery and laden with possibilities for entry into even greater microcosms. Of the telephone, for instance, Benjamin recalled the rupture it caused in the quiet domesticity of family life:

> The sound with which it rang between two and four in the afternoon, when a schoolfriend wished to speak to me, was an alarm signal that menaced not only my parents' midday nap but the historical era that underwrote and enveloped this siesta. Disagreements with switchboard operators were the rule, to say nothing of the threats and curses uttered by my father when he had the complaints department on the line. But his real orgies were reserved for cranking the handle, to which he gave up himself for minutes at a time, nearly

forgetting himself in the process. His hand, on these occasions, was a dervish overcome by frenzy. My heart would pound; I was certain that an employee on the other end was in danger of a stroke, as punishment for her negligence.[112]

Benjamin believed his work to be in the mould of Leibniz's theory of monads, and thus, like others whose engagement with the past was driven towards an examination of fragments and traces (the microhistorian Carlo Ginzburg being another), he saw something akin to the universal in the particular, and held that the small and seemingly insignificant actually carried more weight than broader and more general historical explanations. 'The divining rod' of Benjamin's intuition, Siegfried Kracauer wrote in 1928,

> hits upon the realm of the inconspicuous, upon the realm of the generally deprecated, upon the realm that history has passed over, and it is precisely here that it discovers its greatest significance.[113]

The world of childhood, too, is a suitable complement to any consideration of the importance of small things; it tells us, through our experience of being children, how there do exist microcosms within the larger context of daily life. Children, Benjamin says, create their world 'surrounded by a world of giants', and through almost anything – from toys to the wreckage of construction sites – 'create a world appropriate to their size'.[114] In a consideration of the materiality of children's toys, he noted how even the least promising remnants and leftovers seem to offer the possibility of the magical transformation of the present:

> no one is more chaste in the use of materials than children: a bit of wood, a pinecone, a small stone – however unified and ambiguous the material is, the more of it seems to embrace the possibilities of a multitude of figures of the most varied sort.[115]

It was no accident that Benjamin had focused so much attention on childhood experience and the kind of fascinations that tend to preoccupy children. To still be a child was to be capable of seeing the world anew every day, of willing a kind of repetition that kept demanding to restart and do it all again.

But Benjamin, of course, wrote as a grown man aware that to be consumed by the wonders that might escape the opening of memory's fan was to be essentially incapable of ever being at home in the way that the child exists within some kind of immemorial sphere of security.[116] Those who do not pursue the 'eternal homeland', Benjamin notes, most likely seek 'eternal voyaging'.[117] In either case there is yearning, longing, melancholy. To seek the eternal homeland is akin to seeing the one you love everywhere and in everything:

> And from this it follows that the faculty of imagination is the gift of interpolating into the infinitely small, of inventing, for every intensity, an extensiveness to contain its new, compressed fullness, in short, of receiving each image as if it were that of the folded fan, which only in spreading draws breath and flourishes, in its new expanse, the beloved features within it.[118]

If Benjamin sought, in his childhood reminiscences, to waken 'homesickness . . . to limit its effect through insight into the irretrievability' of the past at the level of something like collective memory, it was nonetheless accompanied by a conviction of the value of childhood thinking for greater social purposes.[119] Society was to be awakened from the myth of progress by what he described as his 'dialectical' fairy tale, the work that has come to be known as the Arcades Project (*Passegen-Werk*). This was Benjamin's never-completed survey of nineteenth-century Paris, which today only exists as the collection of quotations and observations assembled after his death. One scholar who undertook to reconstruct and attempt to 'write out' from Benjamin's fragments and sketches, Susan Buck-Morss, suggests that his work on the Paris arcades was intended to create a rather different kind of relationship to the past than that of history with a capital 'H'. It sought out a 'space of history', she notes, which set itself against what Benjamin saw as the myth of modernity's progress. This 'space of history' thus 'referred not only to the previous century, but to the ontogenetic, "natural" history of childhood – specifically the childhood of his own generation, born at the century's close'.[120] His generation, Benjamin felt, bore a special responsibility for 'reconstructing the capacity for experience' that the trauma of modernity left at the mercy of the dream world of commodities.[121] History as progress reflected the dominant bourgeois ideology. Childhood thinking ran counter to that, for it was drawn to 'valueless, intentionless' things that were overlooked in the adult world, and which in mass culture were now everywhere as the trash of its dream visions, in the accumulation of commodities from bygone eras that were to be found in the Paris arcades. These represented a collective dream of progress that returns as the unconscious. In such a manner, 'new inventions, conceived out of the fantasy of one generation, are received within the childhood experience of another':

> The 'trick' in Benjamin's fairy tale is to interpret out of the discarded dream images of mass culture a politically empowering knowledge of the collective's own unconscious past. He believes he can do this because it is through such objects that the collective unconscious communicates across generations ... At this intersection between collective history and personal history ... the contents of the collective unconscious are transmitted.[122]

If memory is manifested as a social relation – which is to say, in forms too numerous to detail – and exists as a phenomenon that always seems too elusive to adequately objectify it, it is a fact we are arguably first reminded of at the personal level by the process of ageing, which puts distance between now and the past. To reach a point at which one discovers the impact of a lifetime's worth of experience on a sense of the now, is to see in the constellations of memory a point beyond which our power over this past, and therefore over the present and future, gives way to the force of a dormant and distant unconscious history. This may be located in the objects we surround ourselves with – the keepsakes, souvenirs and material stuff of life – as much as in the impulses that drive us and motivate us without our always being aware of or acknowledging them. This is merely to state the obvious fact that there is efficacy in the material world, and it reaches deep into the sense of who we are.

*

WE MIGHT COMMONLY think of the past in terms of images that are at once distant and made available to us by memory. While the prismatic or kaleidoscopic sense of being pulled through time into another sensorium – 'as if down a spy-glass', to quote Wittgenstein – seems to locate a kind of self-recognition in such images of the past, for Walter Benjamin this was far less interesting than the way that materiality of modern life deepened an awareness of the past existing in the present.[123] Benjamin's childhood recollections, Buck-Morss suggests, are the link between an interest in a Proustian involuntary memory and something akin to collective history:

> he retained the notion that the Arcades project would present collective history as Proust had presented his own – not 'life as it was', not even life remembered, but life as it had been 'forgotten'. Like dream images, urban objects, relics of the last century, were hieroglyphic clues to a forgotten past. Benjamin's goal was to interpret for his own generation these dream fetishes in which, in fossilized form, history's traces had survived.[124]

For Harry Harootunian, reflecting on the work of Benjamin and others, the category of the everyday was crucial to grasping the nature of modernity in that it provided a 'minimal unity' of the present, and thus an organizing principle for experience – a means of coping with the 'too-muchness' of a reality always characterized by excess, surfeit, and that which just keeps on coming. It is within that context that one can read Benjamin's elaboration of a historical consciousness awakened through traces as a very particular way of looking at memory. 'This minimal experience of unity', Harootunian wrote,

> is always unsettled by the violence of events that the receiving consciousness disaggregates not as memory as such, but as trace, not as a figured image, but as 'cinders', remains left by

a devastating trauma. These remains roam about like the dead (or perhaps the undead) – what Benjamin once called 'involuntary memory' – who wait for their hour to return among the living and upset the present, like specters waiting to avenge themselves if the present fails to remember them.[125]

Following Freud's development of psychoanalysis, memory has always had a close and undeniably complicated, often controversial relationship with his theory of the unconscious.[126] It seems to be an obvious task to draw some parallels between the two here, before noting that the unconscious in Benjamin also has pre-Freudian roots in eighteenth-century German thinking.

For Freud, memory belonged to the psyche, which harboured an unconscious whose power for most of the time lay dormant, buried under the memory of more recent experience, but which was not eroded by the passage of time. 'Repressed memory traces', he wrote, 'undergo no alteration, even in the largest period of time.'[127] Psychoanalysis, Freud famously thought, had to proceed by way of a kind of archaeological method to get to these buried, or repressed, memories. The outward signs of such memories prior to the work of analysis would emerge fitfully in dreams or in other emanations of the unconscious – nervous tics, slips of the tongue and so on – thus causing distress. Benjamin also used a similar metaphor of surface and depth, and burrowing deep to get at the truth, when he wrote in a fragment titled 'Excavation and Memory' that 'he who seeks to approach his own past must conduct himself like a man digging.'[128]

Benjamin, too, was much taken with the potential of dreams and the phantasmagoric as conduits of a different kind of truth.[129] In one of the numerous aphorisms that are scattered throughout his Arcades Project, he alluded to the kind of dormant forces Freud identified in the psyche when he noted that modernity, too, had its own anterior; 'its antiquity, like a nightmare that has come to it in its sleep.'[130]

But the particular 'unconscious' we see coming through in his fidelity to the suppressed historical remnant is arguably Leibnizian in its appreciation of the infinitesimal, and in revealing, as Kracauer wrote, 'that big matters are small, and small matters are big'.[131] Like Leibniz, Benjamin's thought 'avails itself of the Platonic doctrine of "ideas"', which leads us to consider the unconscious as it emerges in material plenitude, or as the reminiscence of a reality whose immanence is concealed. The unconscious resides also in the experience of modernity as one of shifting temporalities, where the past and present may co-exist alongside the future that is always being born. This, as we have seen, conjures into being its own phantasmagoric dimensions – imaginary pasts and futures – seen from the perspective of a reality that, as Christine Buci-Glucksmann wrote in relation to Benjamin, had 'become enigmatic, hieroglyphic, non-"rational"'.[132]

As one of the principal subjects of Benjamin's reflections, Baudelaire's idea of modernity – in which experience is inextricably bound up with 'the ephemeral, the fugitive, the contingent . . . the forgetting of the past and the acceptance of the immediate' – directs our attention to the peculiar aesthetics of the novel experience.[133] Modern life, for Benjamin, was caught within the kind of 'dream spaces' that made experience of the now the primary condition of urban life, if not experience in capitalist societies in general. Modern 'consciousness', carried along by the ideology of progress, existed in a 'mythic, dream state' which required a 'particular kind of historical knowledge' to break its spell.[134] To the extent that in Baudelaire modernity is 'consciousness of the present as present', memory could no longer be thought of as merely a faculty in the possession of an individual but must be thought of instead as a capacity for historical thinking obscured by the myth of the eternal now, which itself was in denial of the power of death over authentic memory.

In other writings, such as 'The Storyteller', Benjamin considers how information, in the form of the newspaper, represented the new as against 'the epic side of truth and wisdom' embodied in oral tradition and the figure of the storyteller. 'Death is the sanction of everything that the storyteller can tell', he wrote: 'He has borrowed his authority from death.'[135] In other words, it is not history but what Benjamin refers to as 'natural history', which in this case is an awareness of the affinity that the human and the natural attain in the cycles of generation and decay, which illustrates, Eric Santner says, 'that life can persist beyond the symbolic forms that gave it meaning'.[136]

As a response to the uniqueness of this modern experience, Benjamin's renowned and never-completed Arcades Project formulated an 'imagined' version of nineteenth-century Paris as a counterpoint to the apparent 'dream-state' of advanced capitalism. It consisted of the rags, the refuse and the decaying souvenirs that under the prism of a properly attuned historical consciousness could be raised to life. By revisiting the Paris of old in the present, Benjamin sought to harness the power of a collective memory that was remade as an awakened historical demand for change. This type of memory presented a version of history that was a different kind of time tunnel; one built into the very fabric of cities through these nineteenth-century shopping arcades. By extension, we could say, this 'memory' was capable of being found in the most mundane and neglected areas of everyday life, if one could, like a detective, follow the clues. A key phrase in Benjamin's lexicon in this regard is the 'profane illumination' that would bring into view the repetitious cycles of capitalism and, more importantly, a collective revolutionary potential under repression. More particularly, the contents of these nineteenth-century dream spaces – curiosities, antiquities and the leftovers of commodity production – revealed an unusual ecology of memory in the unwanted:

> Here was the last refuge of those infant prodigies that saw the light of day at the time of the world exhibitions: the brief-case with interior lighting, the meter-long pocket knife, or the patented umbrella handle with built-in watch and revolver.[137]

What Benjamin's fascinations reveal is not just an oddly attuned perspective on memory, but how far we have gone into the things with which we temporarily surround ourselves: 'infant prodigies', the allure of all things miniature, the power of toys, the child's fascination with dead stuff and so on. 'He was apt to offer philosophical reflections', Gershom Scholem recalled, 'as he brought forth a toy for his son.'[138] His 'deep, inner relationship to things he owned', it was said, was always connected to an awareness of worlds within worlds.

II

Presences

There is at every moment an infinity of perceptions
within us.
G. W. Leibniz

Take a long and considered look at your surroundings; try to
impress upon your mind the form, shape and detail of the space
that surrounds you. Then close your eyes firmly and try to recall
what you have just taken in. It is tempting to say that you may feel
as if you have just performed a mental exercise that is somewhat akin
to taking a 'photograph' – you 'pictured' the scene around you – yet
it is likely that when you try to call up an image of your surroundings
you don't see much at all, let alone a 'photographic' image that lingers
somewhere behind those closed eyes.

There may be a lag between this act of what we would nonetheless
refer to as picturing and being able to recollect a moment 'photographically', if it can be recollected at all. If we consider the potency
of the Proustian involuntary memory, it arguably lies, as Walter
Benjamin suggested, in the fact that it is 'only what is not experienced
explicitly and consciously' as 'an experience' that takes hold of us
and spins us around.[1] We have all experienced the sensation of glimps-
ing ourselves from a detached perspective that is complicated by a
sense of intimate knowledge; almost as though observing a film in
which we have participated. It is a phenomenon that confirms Paul
Ricoeur's observation that to be conscious at all, in a human sense,
entails being caught within a world of images; and, further, that 'the
presence in which the representation of the past seems to consist
does indeed appear to be that of an image.'[2]

The Mirror of Reality

How, then, Ricoeur wonders, are we to comprehend the nature of 'an absent thing' – which is to say, just such an image, or a person, or even a sensation – that is at once a presence that is nonetheless indelibly 'stamped with the seal of the anterior?'[3] How, in other words, can we be in the present and in the past all at once? One answer to such a question had earlier been found in Henri Bergson's *Matter and Memory*, one of the first post-photographic considerations of memory. For Bergson, the 'dead weight' of the past – or, in other words, memory – is seen to relate to the present through 'the unconscious'.[4] The past, that is to say, is not in the mind, ordered and under command; the mind, rather, is a receptor through which images of the past come in to the present.

This describes one more source of a multitemporal existence, and it is more than simply an effect of living in a post-photographic world – or even a post-cinematic world – where the analogy between thought and memory is most readily applied to a conception of photographic forms and processes, even if this is to point to the enigmatic or mysterious power of memory. Perhaps reflecting how commonplace such thinking is, Friedrich Kittler bluntly states that

> In 1900, the soul suddenly stopped being a memory in the form of wax slates or books, as Plato describes it; rather, it was technically advanced and transformed into a motion picture.[5]

What happened at the turn of the twentieth century to explain this sudden apparent transformation in the nature of memory was the development of cinematic photography. This, Kittler argues, just happened to be accompanied by a peculiar phenomenon that seemed essentially cinematic itself, or at least took its cue from the language of cinema: the near-death experience that seemed to be always accompanied by 'a rapid time-lapse film of an entire life projected once again in the mind's eye'.[6]

More to the point, however, is that the category of the image takes us into the mind of the human itself. Thus history shows that *thoughts* and *ideas* have mostly been considered in terms of picturing, and the mind often compared to a medium of visual representation. Bergson, indeed, suggested that we direct our attention to the world in the manner of a camera, taking snapshots of a reality in continual flux.[7]

Bergson's statement that 'perception and memory begin in photography' might seem to be a strange claim that identifies him as a thinker overly influenced by the revolution that the new technology had wrought in his own lifetime – that of the late nineteenth century – but such an understanding sought to point to a mode of perceiving that was in many ways comparable to the optical mechanism underlying photography, but which nonetheless pre-dated the technology of the camera by some considerable time. It was an analogy that reached back to the ancient Greek notion of *eidos* – or, 'the stable view taken of the instability of things' – which itself pointed to the importance of image-like impressions to consciousness.[8] Bergson's ideas about memory thus posit the significance of 'a photography before photography as we know it'.[9] Perception, Bergson thought, operates in a speedy and efficient manner because it is always suffused with prior perceptions that are located in memory; thus 'with the immediate and present data of our senses we mingle a thousand details out of our past experience', leading to the possible confusion of past and present:

> In most cases these memories supplant our actual perceptions, of which we then retain only a few hints, thus using them merely as 'signs' that recall to us former images. The convenience and the rapidity of perception are bought at this price; but hence also springs every kind of illusion.[10]

This may be why the 'snapshot' I – or you – have just taken cannot immediately be conjured up in the imagination, but instead may appear – involuntarily – at some point in the future as a kind of flashback, or an unwelcome, ghostly apparition, produced by smells, sounds, tastes and other senses. The most celebrated literary example of this is to be found in Marcel Proust's *In Search of Lost Time*. In the well-known account of a phenomenon probably known to everyone, the narrator – also named Marcel – lingers on 'the image, the visual memory' that stirs within when he tastes the madeleine dipped in tea, which carries him back in time, immersing him in a vivid childhood tableau:

> Immediately the old grey house upon the street . . . rose up like a stage set to attach itself to the little pavilion opening on to the garden . . . the whole of Combray and its surroundings, taking shape and solidity, sprang into being, town and gardens alike from my cup of tea.[11]

Beyond this particular example, Joshua Landy notes, Proust's multi-volume novel plays through the experience of involuntary memory as a facet of everyday life. We see that this 'Proustian' capacity for picturing one's past is 'subject to the vicissitudes of human consciousness', which is not a mechanism like a camera, actively wielded like a kind of sensory weapon taking snapshots, but the very stuff – the Bergsonian flux – that self-consciousness might attempt to arrest or direct. This is to say that memory as an involuntary consciousness overwhelmed by images is found to be 'flowing freely when unbidden, ebbing as soon as summoned'.[12]

The attempt to grasp this world in motion would lead others – such as William Henry Fox Talbot, one of the inventors of the camera – to describe the new apparatus as the pencil of nature, recording more accurate impressions of a world that was constantly changing than painting or earlier forms of representation could. While we might easily consider photography to be yet one more way in which memory is inscribed – much like writing on paper, or sound recording – and which, in terms of Pierre Nora's notion of *lieux de mémoire*, is something that in a modern and, particularly, contemporary archival culture becomes a proxy for memory. The idea of what an image (and a memory-image) may in essence be informs more profoundly our understanding of consciousness, and how it in turn produces memory. It should perhaps then not be a surprise to note the prevalence and persistence of certain image or picture metaphors in thinking about the nature of consciousness and memory. Among the metaphors for memory employed by Plato, that of writing is most commonly noted, but, as M. H. Abrams commented, to 'elucidate the nature of sense perception, memory and thought', Plato did also think of paintings as metaphors for memory and, indeed, 'appealed to the reflection of images in a mirror'.[13] Since the seventeenth century in particular, which is to say before the invention of photography as we know it today, this is an analogy that has often been repeated, or altered in ways that reflected developments in optics. As Locke insisted in *An Essay Concerning Human Understanding* (originally published in 1689), the effect of sensations on the understanding – the way in which, for instance, the world enters our very being as this phenomenon we call *idea* – is much like a light or projection that illuminates a dark room. This room, located somewhere in the mind, is thus little more than a kind of camera obscura that reflects the external world as a picture-image. 'The *understanding* is not much unlike a closet wholly shut from light, with only some little opening left', Locke wrote:

> to let in external visible resemblances, or ideas of things without; would the pictures coming into such a dark room but stay there, and lie so orderly as to be found upon occasion, it would very much resemble the understanding of a man in reference to all objects of sight and the *ideas* of them.[14]

Both Descartes, who preceded Locke, 'and the *philosophes* influenced by Locke remained beholden to a concept of the mind as a camera obscura'.[15] In the *Dioptrics*, a treatise on the nature of light, vision and lenses, Descartes suggested that a simple experiment that involved placing an eye in the hole in the camera obscura that lets in the light could show how vision worked:

> Take an eye of a newly dead man (or failing that, of an ox or some other large animal); carefully cut away the three enveloping membranes at the back so as to expose a large part of the humour without shedding any; then cover the hole with some white body, thin enough to let the daylight through (e.g., a piece of paper or an eggshell). Now put this eye in the hole of a specially made shutter, so that its front faces a spot where there are a number of objects lit up by the sun, and the back

Illustration of two children looking at a table camera obscura, from A. Ganot (1804–1887), *Natural Philosophy*. A camera obscura is a box, or darkened room, with a lens or hole through which the image of an external object is projected on to the opposite inside wall. The devices were known to the ancient Chinese and Greeks, and used by Arab astronomers in the 10th century to observe the sun and by artists during the Renaissance to create accurate drawings.

where the white body is, faces the inside of the room you are in. (No light must enter the room except through the eye . . .) if you now look at the white body, you will see (I dare say with surprise and pleasure) a picture representing in natural perspective all the objects outside . . . Further the images of objects are not only produced in the back of the eye but also sent on to the brain.[16]

Earlier still, and in more arcane circles, the 'Oculus Imaginationis' – the inner eye (the mind or memory) – was understood to direct the light of the external world on to a 'screen of fantasy, hovering at somewhere beyond the back of the head'.[17]

But the mental images early modern thinkers described are no less phantasmic; manifestations of incorporeal forces or powers that seem to hold sway over human agency and ingenuity. Thus in his *Meditations* Descartes supposed the existence of some malignant demon who was feeding him dreamlike illusions that called his knowledge of the world into doubt, 'laying snares for my credulity'.[18] 'I suppose . . . that all the things which I see are false (fictitious)', Descartes wrote. 'I believe that none of these objects which my fallacious memory represents ever existed.'[19]

With the addition of technical aids to perception, particularly those of the nineteenth century such as the camera and the phonograph, the idea that visual sensations could be misleading gained momentum, perhaps in part because new optical technologies had in fact seemed to prove devastatingly effective, revealing more of the world than ever before. The developments in optics in the early modern period had already revolutionized the human understanding and enlarged the dominion of knowledge: both the heavens and the molecular world were exposed (by the telescope and microscope, respectively), in turn recontextualizing the limits and understanding of a human subjectivity that with each advance seemed to become less significant. In the face of such apparent reconfigurations of reality, the nature and scope of memory as an organizer of knowledge and guarantor of the fiction we know of as 'self' was thrown into relief. As a result, memory could only be seen as, at once, a quality or capacity of the self *and* – importantly – of the various technologies that now supplemented it.

Under the influence of the transformations modernity had made to the character of daily life – the overstimulation of the senses, and the aesthetic appreciation of a world in flux – and before the emergence of photography, the connection between sensory perception and memory had been coming under closer scrutiny. Toys and gadgets, such as 'the thaumatrope, or "wonder-turner" (demonstrating the effect of after-images)', Daniel Pick writes, became part and parcel of 'more erudite philosophical and aesthetic speculations about perception' that reflected on the potentially overwhelming nature of a world that technology revealed as having seemingly boundless dimensions.[20] Thus notable thinkers of the day wrote about how we necessarily 'fend off as well as take in an unmanageable stream of sensory inputs'.[21] The impossibility of holding back the world of sense was much later drawn out and fantastically exaggerated by Jorge Luis Borges in his short story 'Funes the Memorious'. Here we glimpse a young man who was unable to shut off a world that was experienced as a continual sensory assault, thus giving him the apparent ability to 'remember' everything. He lived a life of always looming sensory tumult, and was ultimately reduced to a living wreck before finally being overcome by the force of the world. 'He was', Borges writes, 'the solitary, lucid spectator of a multiform, momentaneous and almost unbelievably precise world . . . he had more memories than all of mankind since the world began.'[22]

Faced with a world seemingly expanding in depth and magnitude, the problem in historical terms became not just one of how 'the mind extracts as well as obscures other images in order to perceive', but how memory itself – now aided by an abundance of technical means and add-ons – could finally capture and preserve something akin to truth.[23] Yet it seems that developments in technology, outpaced by visions of the future, were merely catching up with an eternal desire for a kind of visual recognition that might encompass reality as a re-presentation of somewhere known and familiar; a place where we understand ourselves to be at home. Influenced by the power of memory to 'preserve certain events from oblivion', John Berger noted, 'nearly all cultures have assumed that there was somewhere an all-seeing eye'.[24] Where once we 'accredited this eye to spirits, ancestors, Gods, or a single God', it can now be found, for instance, in photography, which has come to be used as just such 'an all-seeing eye', recording events, preserving places, picturing loved ones and describing a reality that might otherwise vanish forever.[25]

Awash as our environment is today with the products of photography, whose images grace surfaces all around us and whose vast archives have been shrunk into pocket-sized devices, the notion that consciousness and memory can be understood partly in terms of *images* that are photographic or filmic in nature retains its hold precisely because the use of the image metaphor to refer to thinking, to ideas and, indeed, to consciousness pre-dates the forms through which experience is mediated today. It fits our most common-sense ways of describing perception; the technical advances or accomplishments, by contrast – like a newly discovered country filled with unfamiliar plant and animal species – merely reinforce the power of the metaphor. What this means, though, is that the philosophical problems around the reliability of what the visual sense provides to memory are not resolved by our greater acquaintance with visual technologies, but are only made more complex. Thus while Bergson's idea that perception was akin to a 'kind of photographic view of things', in which unknown 'chemical or psychical processes' develop something like a photograph in the mind, might force us to consider how these technical aids tend towards an increasingly *private* view of the world, it would be wrong to overlook the fact that impersonal images often seem to us to be at one with what we take to be personal memory. As such, photography enlarges the scope of cultural or collective memory. Even when their images are 'divorced from all first-hand experience', Berger argues, 'photographers are agents of memory'.[26]

This, of course, throws us into a richly promiscuous visual realm of uncontrollable, fleeting phenomena; one that is imaginatively informed – or swayed by passion and even lacking credulity – in something akin to the way Descartes supposed when he posited the existence of the evil demon fuelling his thoughts. For Maurice Halbwachs, a one-time student of Bergson's whose writings laid the groundwork for sociological studies of collective memory, getting too caught up in the picture-image metaphor of memory could lead into the realm of dreams, which he took to be precisely opposed to memory. For Halbwachs memory was rather something that came to life through a variety of social frameworks – which is to say, it was embodied in the shared experience of place, habit and language.[27]

If that suggests a conception of memory that roots it in the reality of day-to-day life, all memory is nonetheless virtual in the sense that it mirrors reality or mirrors experience. Even collective life, as we will see, reflects the 'myths' that bind people together. All memory, in a sense, is virtual. It is called to presence, or rises to the surface to claim our attention. It was not until Bergson's *Matter and Memory*, published at the turn of the twentieth century, that the visual realm was thought of in terms of the 'virtual'. It is a term that we are used to associating with simulations of reality and computer-mediated technologies that produce 'virtual reality', but for Bergson the mere fact that 'the past remains with us, and yet is in actuality no longer present' identifies recollection – and thus memory – with virtuality.[28] For Gilles Deleuze, Bergson tells us that 'memory is the real name of the relation to oneself, or the affect on self by self.' This is to say that memory is not merely remembering (patchy, willed, resistant to efforts at recall) but indeed is 'the "absolute memory" which doubles the present'.[29]

Shadows and Light

If memory – or the capacity for recollection – might, in this sense, be thought of as an instrument that permits a kind of time travel into hidden depths that charts the transformation of the real into the virtual, and where the conscious world melts into the melange of the unconscious, it is a notion that in different language can be seen to reach all the way back to the Homeric poems. The richness of these works within the development of Western culture up to and through modernity accounts in part for their power in allowing us to see how we have thought and continue to think about the line between the individual and the world he or she inhabits, and, no less, what lies beyond it, or even opposed to it. Taken by themselves, these stories are archetypes – images – of the human condition. The *Odyssey's* account of the mythical return of its hero, for instance – the so-called *nostos* (return home) from which we derive our word 'nostalgia' – may be the earliest known (if not also the most notable) of all literary treatments of the subject of memory and its centrality to an understanding of the human condition as it relates to ideas of home and the homeland. The *Odyssey's* underworld, Hades, has been described as 'the ultimate topos of memory, a kind of memoria conceived as the deepest and most hidden recesses of the mind'.[30] But, more significantly, the relation of memory to image and image to unconscious is already there in a way that Freud, for instance, recognized when he observed that dreams and, indeed, memories 'constitute the mental underworld, the nucleus of the true unconscious', which in turn stimulates an archaic or animal heritage that is commonly expressed in myths that allow for the dramatic working through of repressed thoughts.[31]

Indeed, one is tempted to say that the dead of the ancient under-world – a place characterized as a shadowy realm – are conjured up in terms that today suggest the flickering holograms or computer-generated simulations of new media technologies; they are the real that is yet not real, the trace of the actual we would call – in a general sense – virtual. The dead are thus 'shades' or shadows (psyches, or souls) – sometimes also described as 'images' – which are illuminated when they come into contact with the world of the living, just as if they had survived bodily death and on these occasions flicker into some kind of half-life. For the ancient Greeks – and we see this in the *Odyssey* – the psyche, or soul, departed the body at the time of death. These shades that remain lingering in the underworld, escape 'out of the mouth – or out of the gaping wound of the dying.'[32] As Erwin Rohde wrote, 'the soul' therefore persists, but as a mere reflection of what it once was:

> now freed from its prison [the soul] becomes, as the name well expresses it, an 'image'. On the borders of Hades Odysseus sees floating 'the images of those that have toiled (on earth)'. These immaterial images withdrawing themselves from the grasp of the living, like smoke or a shadow . . . present the general outlines of the once living person.[33]

The significance of these Homeric shadows to this discussion could easily be dismissed as a mere literary device, serving only to draw our attention to the ways in which photography – and, later, film – would come to establish some kind of living connection to the dead, much in the way that shades or 'images' did in myth. Yet the link illustrates the power within imagination and memory of the no-longer living, but still lingering, whether it comes in the form of a photograph or some other image that perhaps points to the real presence of an unconscious or involuntary memory. This connec-tion to the unconscious implicates human experience in a temporal dimension that goes in a different direction from a progressive time that is always extending into the future. We learn, as the ancients knew, that human experience is split three ways: into past, present and future. It is mediated, furthermore, by the hold that images, as they relate to memory, have on the imagination, and the capacity they have for drawing us back into an interior that rises to the surface in unexpected and unpredictable ways.

Where visitors to the underworld provoked the appearance of the dead through the rites of a sacrificial offering – in a kind of drama that stops the world spinning on its axis long enough to allow the living to step into the shadows – we moderns might be said to perform a similar kind of trick through our unthinking resort to mediated images, to simulations and to the lure of the visual. These now populate our reality to the extent that the world they give rise to appears as natural as the unadorned imagination that was once presumed to light the interior world did to the premoderns. Thus our images – and it seems to be true of photographs, in particular – never entirely vanish; they have material form, they are things we have around us, mementoes we carry on our person. But, in mediating the realms of the living and the dead, so to speak, they may simply ensure that the departed, as W. G. Sebald remarked, always seem to 'hover somewhere at the perimeter of our lives'.[34] And as these 'representations' become more vivid and lifelike through developments in visual technologies, and more immersive in the encounters they permit, they draw us further into what we might call a mythical temporality, which is multifaceted and ruled by unconscious forces that appear in the form of traces, both material and mental.

One might point to numerous examples in contemporary culture that could illustrate this; instances that seem to mimic the Homeric association between memory and the unconscious. One vivid example that, in some of its detail, recalls Odysseus' visit to the underworld can be found in the Steven Spielberg movie *Minority Report* (2002, based on a short story of 1956 by Philip K. Dick). The central character in the film, a police officer named John Anderton (played by Tom Cruise), is captain of the so-called PreCrime Division, which has found the means to see far enough into the future, using strange premonitions – or unnatural *forward* 'recollections' of a kind, relating to events yet to unfold in reality but already predetermined – to prevent crimes before they happen. Anderton himself is the chief advocate of its methods until he himself happens to be fingered as a murderer-in-waiting. As he goes on the run from his fate – a future inextricably bound to his present conditions, and to events in his past that provide him with a motive for the crime he seems destined to commit – he is drawn, as Odysseus was drawn to the underworld, to the burial place of memory. Here it is conjured up in the insubstantial holographic form of his lost son and estranged wife. They belong at once to a time and a place and a set of circumstances long since vanished, yet one also capable of being brought uncannily into the now. Imagination, longing and the memory of a better time are what sustain Anderton's attachment to the trauma of his own past, but it is only through the virtual embodiment of his loved ones – like the dead of the *Odyssey*, raised back to some kind of half-life – who break into his reality in three-dimensional, insubstantial, 'fluttering' form. Where Odysseus made a sacrifice to enter the underworld, Anderton ingests a mysterious and illegal drug before calling up the images on a media console, which restores him temporarily to his past life. Like the *Odyssey*, *Minority Report* illustrates ritualized enactments of memory and the lure of absent presences. Were Anderton to reach out to embrace his son, his arms would

John Anderton plays the holographic image of his lost child in *Minority Report* (dir. Steven Spielberg, 2002).

merely grasp at that which looks almost alive, but might as well be a shadow.

The scene also draws our attention, through the suspicion that Anderton is a drug addict, to a relationship not touched on in this discussion so far: the importance of repetition to memory, and the relation to habit. We conceive of the drug addict, David Lenson remarks, as one who is characteristically driven by a desire that can never be satisfied, and which thus produces the repetition compulsion. It is in this respect that such a 'drug' – and speaking loosely this might include anything with the potential to open up other words, such as Proust's madeleine – mediates the attempt at recollection. Even happy memories, thus revisited with the aid of substances that switch the user into the realm of the atemporal, can quickly become their opposite. Along with the promise of oblivion, 'they bring with them their own kind of pain', Lenson writes:

> The pleasure of a happy memory . . . is self-negating. The shades wandering the floor of the old Greek Hades had forgetfulness as the object of their quest. Blackout – what many of us fear most among the myths of death – was previsioned as a state of grace for them. Their condition is a metaphor for memory.[35]

And so, in *Minority Report*, Anderton seeks to both remember and forget. It is perhaps worth making the point here that our tendency to relate the idea of the virtual to virtual reality simulations produced by media technologies can lead us to lose contact with the Bergsonian notion of the virtual – in a nutshell it is internal, and it relates to memory; it is this that can be seen in its connection to the kind of narcotic reverie I have just been discussing. Hillel Schwartz, for instance, reminds us that whatever else we think the virtual is, it is 'the hallucination of heaven, the peyote vision, the dionysiac stupor' and, indeed, 'any system devised for losing ourselves in another world'.[36] So-called virtual reality, in other words, is a destination reached by many routes.

What we hold against the drug addict who is lured into this half-world is that they seem able to cut themselves off from the world, to take 'exile from reality', as Jacques Derrida remarked:

[The drug user] escapes into a world of simulacrum and fiction. He is reproached for something like his taste in hallucinations . . . We do not object to the drug user's pleasure per se, but to a pleasure taken in an experience without truth.[37]

This apparent act of bringing the past to some kind of half-life has, as we have seen already, moved beyond the particularity of the personal encounter, or a personal connection with, for instance, photographs. Beyond the intimate sense of nostalgia, images clearly also mediate public memory, which is itself sustained by memorials and museums, and the more recent phenomenon of 'postmemory'. Marianne Hirsch, whose writing has done much to explore and develop this notion, distinguishes it – as a kind of memory – from the personal by arguing that it is not, like the memory we suppose to give unity to a self, the product of an 'identity position'; rather it is 'a space of remembrance, more broadly available through cultural and public, and not merely individual and personal, acts of remembrance, identification, and projection'.[38] We might note, too, that images and representations that seek in such a way to reconstitute some idea of the past are central to what Pierre Nora has termed *lieux de mémoire* – roughly meaning those spaces (museums, exhibitions) filled with 'vestiges' and 'illusions of eternity' that towards the end of the twentieth century began to appear as substitutes for memory, thereby creating a new phenomenon that is, 'first of all, archival'.[39]

Lieux de mémoire arise out of a sense that there is no such thing as spontaneous memory, hence that we must create archives, mark anniversaries, organize celebrations . . .[40]

If the phenomenon of memory is itself – in its various manifestations, and supported by innumerable props and stand-ins – the index of an absent present, or the strange and yet familiar, it is no less the evidence of a capacity we can understand at the subjective level to be both active and passive. Doubtless, then, whatever mediates or stands between the two poles of such oppositions becomes invested with a high degree of magic; a transformative capacity that in a sense can switch us on and off, or allow us to slip in and out of a consciously constructed present now made porous, to metaphorically move between two worlds. 'The trace', Pierre Nora notes, 'negates the sacred but retains its aura.'[41] Hence the allure of involuntary memory in its most well-known account by Proust; there Marcel finds pleasure in various modes of passivity that border on non-being or self-negation: sleep, dreams and reverie,

> a desire for some release from the burdens of 'waking' agency that introduces the recurring images of passivity and its many pleasures: being pursued, being a beloved . . . being made an object.[42]

Yet we may have become so accustomed to materialized, mediated images that we will not permit the realization that something like a photograph, or the moving images contained in a film, is a token with the power to compel us to switch worlds; to embark on a journey that proceeds inwards to reconnect with what should have vanished, what might never have been there and what is irretrievably lost, and – not least – to indulge in a kind of time travel that dissolves reality.

Reflecting on the spell photography might cast over the fugitive forms of reality, William Henry Fox Talbot wrote in 1839 that as he glanced at the world around him with this mechanical eye, even 'the most transitory of things' could be fixed for an eternity. Indeed, what could be more emblematic of the close association between being and its attempt to step ahead of itself (to step into experience) than those strange and ungraspable companions we know as our shadows?

> A shadow, the proverbial emblem of all that is fleeting and momentary, may be fettered by the spells of our 'natural magic', and may be fixed forever in the position which it seemed only destined for a single instant to occupy.[43]

Perhaps photography – 'a neat slice of time, not a flow', as Susan Sontag observed – more than any other medium, has come to serve such a purpose.[44] It populates our reality with the forms and figures of that which in actuality was always destined to be no more. Fox Talbot's use of the term 'natural magic' repeats a much earlier description that was applied to the effects of the camera obscura by Renaissance figures, such as the Jesuit polymath Athanasius Kircher, who were known to dabble with occult forces. Where the camera obscura seemed capable of pulling an external view into a new kind of life, both separate and dependent on the world beyond the darkroom, photography fixed things more permanently, establishing everywhere, Marina Warner notes, 'former selves and the presence of people as they were when they were alive'.[45]

While writers, philosophers and scientists have probed the nature of technologies that seem to embody a kind of non-human consciousness, it would be accurate to say that at the level of everyday life we are apt to underestimate or overlook the effect that something as seemingly benign and commonplace as photography has had on us; and particularly on how it invades consciousness and expands memory, melding the subjective trace, imaginative and particular, with a public and social kind of remembrance whose intentions might always have been obscure. To consider the image as it supplements external reality – rounding out memory, filling in gaps in recollection – is to make it into something far removed from a purely archival understanding of the technology and its products, which would give more weight to the storehouse, the repository of information, the book of images and so on, in the constitution of an impersonal *lieu de mémoire*. While the camera and photography constituted 'the most extraordinary technical innovation in vision during the nineteenth century, indeed perhaps in all human history', its impact was precisely contained in its capacity to enlarge consciousness and, as such, to remake the world as a new and strange object of possible experience.[46] But for the keenest and most astute observers of the human condition in the age of technology, such as Walter Benjamin, this was a revolution quickly assimilated in habit and gesture; one that could therefore become almost automatic – just like flicking a lighter to fire up a cigarette.

That kind of analogy allowed Benjamin to hone in on what was easily overlooked: the way that small, jerky and reflexive actions – perhaps unremarkable in themselves – came to find a unity with the passing glances that characterized modern urban life, and which drew the eyes of the one armed with a camera. In 'one abrupt movement of the hand', Benjamin observed, 'the "snapping" of the photographer has had the greatest consequences' on how we relate to the world, and to time:

> A touch of the finger now sufficed to fix an event for an unlimited period of time. The camera gave the moment a posthumous shock, as it were ... Baudelaire speaks of a man who plunges into the crowd as into a reservoir of electric energy. Circumscribing the experience of the shock, he calls this man 'a *kaleidoscope* equipped with consciousness'.[47]

Baudelaire's sense of the city allows us to gain a perspective on the motives of Paris photographers who would mingle with the crowds, searching out the new poetics of urban life amid a sensory assault that prevented 'the impact of particular experiences from becoming assimilated, processed, and remembered'.[48] More broadly, though, his was a recognition that this technique of observing revealed the world to have dizzying depths that would be informed by a consciousness attuned to the very *unconscious* forces that permeated the fabric of social life.

As an invention of the nineteenth century taken up by a new kind of urban flâneur, the camera – as a kind of super-prop, a sensor for the new prosthetic memory – seemed to have arrived just in time, finding itself in a world whose upheavals, for Walter Benjamin, had caused a rupture between the individual and 'collective, inherited memory'.[49] Proust's involuntary memory, he thought, emerged from the isolated experience of modernity, which made the formation of a stable self-image – of identity as memory – a matter of chance; something that might be provoked or prodded into some kind of vital existence by numerous unknowns. By contrast, in a time not yet subject to such modern upheavals in experience – that is to say, still marked by tradition – memory remains tied to the collective:

> The rituals with their ceremonies, their festivals (quite probably recalled nowhere in Proust's work) kept producing the

amalgamation of the two elements of memory over and over again. They triggered recollection at certain times and remained handles of memory for a lifetime. In this way, voluntary and involuntary recollection lose their mutual exclusiveness.[50]

For Baudelaire, the writer who had such an influence on Benjamin, modernity famously gave existence to an art that would be found 'within the tension between the transitory and the eternal'.[51] That tension is revealed – crystallized – in *the moment*, 'which has no reference to other units of time, but', Christoph Asendorf says, 'simultaneously creates for [that particular moment] a continuous temporal dimension by petrifying it and thereby rendering it accessible to memory'.[52] Even when the phenomena captured by the camera have escaped a human eye drawn by other distractions, they give themselves up to the forensic gaze of the mechanized eye. 'The photograph', Roland Barthes notes – situating it in a struggle between life and death – 'mechanically repeats what could never be repeated existentially.'[53] And this, we might presume, is the source of the uncanny we find in the image, or photograph, that accidentally catches our attention.

Thus, of all the arts, photography would seem to capture modernity's passing flux in snapshots that seem to promise – in the terms of Baudelaire's prescription for an art of memory – to 'see all and forget nothing'.[54] In these terms, *seeing* itself, Sontag wrote, when specifically 'pursued' through photography, 'with sufficient avidity and single-mindedness, could reconcile the claims of truth and the need to find the world beautiful'.[55] To look was to make a world, and – in some way – to remember that world *as* an act of making. But lurking in the transitory, as captured in image form, is death. As Sontag commented, 'all photographs are *memento mori*':

> To take a photograph is to participate in another person's (or thing's) mortality, vulnerability, mutability. Precisely by slicing out this moment and freezing it, all photographs testify to time's relentless melt.[56]

This, for Roland Barthes, was the most irreducible truth about these kinds of images.[57] In his well-known meditation on photography, *Camera Lucida*, he pursued the relationship between death, photography and memory. Taken as a form of evidence, or witness to the past, the photograph signalled in the most basic sense that there was once something that we now perhaps can know only through its absence. Photographs thus work to compress time and distance, as the historian Raphael Samuel realized when he first encountered a collection of criminal mug shots relating to a period in the past that had hitherto remained lost in time, but now, in the light of this new evidence, seemed to be invigorated with a fresh life force. 'The faces which stared out at us were startlingly modern,' he recalls, 'with nothing except for the captions – and the criminal record – to indicate that they belonged to the nineteenth century rather than our own.' Those pictured – what he found were the faces of men – were 'clean shaven, with not a sideburn to be seen.'[58] The discovery gave life to a presence that seemed to be dramatically at odds with expectations of what the period style was – the mutton-chopped and be-hatted figures of Victorian fiction and painting, perhaps – at once unmaking the past and remaking it anew.

It is the details, often unexpected or contrary to received wisdom, that animate such apparent visitations from some vanished world. Because the photograph often captures configurations of the real through chance or accident – in evanescent moments, in apparently insubstantial phenomena, like the shadows that caught Fox Talbot's attention – it preserves a level of detail that mere unaided memory might never hope to retain, establishing the grounds for 'a cult of remembrance of loved ones, absent or dead'.[59]

This all relates, no doubt, to the fact that the photographic images themselves become metaphors for our own past experiences. In one desperate moment when he was seemingly on the verge of suicide, Walter Benjamin composed a speech in which he proclaimed memory to consist of a series of proto-cinematic images that open up the personal past to examination. The 'images of life whirring through a dying man's head', he wrote, were like one of those miniature picture books or 'thumb-cinemas' that on other occasions people might flick through at leisure.[60] It seems the most obvious response to the fact that photography often captured the most transitory of experiences that were later cast in a new light by recollection. Recollection always takes place now, in a present that is distant from the thing recalled. 'This is clearest in the case of images in which we see ourselves as we do in dreams', Benjamin wrote:

> We stand before ourselves just as we once stood in an originary past that we never saw. And precisely the most important images – those developed in the darkroom of the lived moment – are what we see . . . the 'whole life' of the person whose life is threatened is composed precisely of these little images. They present a rapid succession, like those precursors of cinematography, the little booklets in which, as children, we could admire a boxer, a swimmer, or a tennis player in action.[61]

Benjamin points to the conundrum of apparently seeing ourselves in a way that suggests we are both participant and observer, as if looking on already from some anticipated afterlife. Roland Barthes reported a similar experience in *Camera Lucida,* baffled by a photograph of himself that he had no memory of appearing in a photographer's exhibition. 'Because it was a photograph I could not deny that I had been *there* (even if I did not know *where*)':

> This distortion between certainty and oblivion gave me a kind of vertigo, something of a 'detective' anguish . . . I went to the photographer's show as to a police investigation, to learn at last what I no longer know about myself.[62]

This kind of strangeness seems peculiarly apparent when we confront images of ourselves, Barthes wrote elsewhere. 'Even and especially for your own body', he wrote in the autobiographical *Roland Barthes,* 'you are condemned to the repertoire of its images . . . you never see your eyes unless they are dulled by the gaze they rest upon the mirror or the lens'. Others, though, see our eyes, see us, as we see them – vivid and lifelike.[63] To look in such a way, to look photographically, that is, is thus to produce the effect of death. 'Photography may correspond to the intrusion, in our modern society, of an asymbolic Death', Barthes claimed: 'a kind of abrupt drive into literal Death . . . reduced to a simple click'.[64]

The Density of Reality

If the absence that turns out to be preserved by the photographic image illustrates, in one way, the presence of death, it equally provides the window into a world that may suddenly appear to thicken with mysteries and to be replete with phenomena that are less easy to reconcile with the personal memory of events that may have been consciously sought out with the lens of the camera.

As I write I am looking at a series of photographs of Los Angeles taken in the 1930s, which astonish because of the sense of time and place – they suggest a world in transit, disappearing almost as it takes form – which is often unintentionally captured in the background details and surroundings of particular places, and in the dress and demeanour of persons who were more likely the object of the photographer's attention than what we might think of as the accidents that happen to hold interest to posterity. An anonymous photograph taken in 1935 of Los Angeles police chief James 'Two Gun' Davis and his gun squad portrays not only its contemporary and probably intended message, that these were men who were prepared to meet criminal violence with equal force, but also something more insubstantial. It is *there*, nonetheless, and perhaps more evocative because like involuntary memory, it is fed by vestiges that float free of historical and experiential moorings.

In this image there is a look and feel that seems to belong to a highly aestheticized Hollywood characterization of law enforcement that is familiar to most of us from numerous movies. The men, with their neat and careful haircuts, shiny shoes and mostly stylish attire, superficially capture a sense of modernity and its fleeting fashions. In this way, the image furnishes details for posterity; which is to say, for some other greater public or historical memory that reaches far beyond the mere memento that the image likely was to its subjects. In banal terms, of course, the sight of these men tells us with fascinating precision what people looked like there and then. But there's

Los Angeles Police Department 'gun squad', 1936.

more. With the benefit of historical distance, and an awareness of the Los Angeles Police Department's reputation for ruthlessness (informed also, no doubt, by numerous Hollywood fictions), the benign, country-club air of the setting – one policeman sports plus-fours, as if taking a break from a game of golf – might easily be overwhelmed by the atmosphere of latent violence. Here, perhaps, we see the sensibilities and mores of the Old West persisting in a new, modern setting. This is photography as unintentional cultural memory.

It is clear that to make such a reading of this artefact is to situate this image within a conception of memory that rests on a world of associations that are supplied in the present, and partially by the viewer; associations that the anonymous photographer could have had little sense of when the scene was immortalized. This image now becomes evidence to embroider a view of that particular time and place with the kind of detail and associations that may have been unremarkable to the contemporary eye. Thus the camera, Benjamin declared, 'introduces us to unconscious optics as does psychoanalysis to unconscious impulses', which means that a great power of observation finds itself within the intentionless mechanism of this strange eye: 'evidently a different nature opens itself to the camera than opens to the naked eye – if only because an unconsciously permeated space is substituted for a space consciously explored.'[65] This unconscious is betrayed in the image that freezes a scene, an event, therefore making it available to a more forensic level of consideration and possibly detection. Yet in so doing it expands the storehouse of information and knowledge that might constitute (or disrupt and undo) our own sense of the past, or what we commonly refer to as memory.

Benjamin's notion of the optical unconscious is expertly dramatized as a metaphysical puzzle in Michelangelo Antonioni's film *Blow-Up* (1966). Featuring not just a photographer as a central character but also the camera itself as a reality-penetrating and alienating device that throws personal memory into doubt, it was a film that suggested 'the treacherous nature of the photograph as evidence, its intrusive and distorting character, and its potential to abstract its maker and its subject from tangible reality'.[66]

In fact, the film plays with the nature of reality on a number of levels that tell us much about memory, in particular how it disrupts the evidence of the senses, and how it can and cannot be represented. Set in the fashion milieu of 'Swinging London', it follows a period of roughly 24 hours in the life of a photographer named Thomas (played by David Hemmings), who we quickly learn is disillusioned with the flat and superficial world of his commercial fashion work. As an adjunct to this world, he is set on producing images that reflect more on the brutality of life that assails the human condition at the margins of society, in a city that behind the pop cultural excess looks as if it has just emerged from the Second World War. Seeking out what late Victorians would have termed the residuum, or leftovers, of time's relentless progress – the almost forgotten London of doss-houses, street traders, urban ruins and abattoirs – the character of Thomas moves between two worlds: the underworld of the mythologized London of pop culture and its chimera. This in particular seems to be what Antonioni was keen to expose, and it is especially evident in the way the film throws up reminders of the fact that even by the mid-1960s the city was still in the process of postwar reconstruction. Thus, as Thomas drives around town, modernist towers and new concrete edifices are seen to rise in the distance, but the foreground is often dominated by rubble-strewn patches of land, as though the

Blitz had been a recent event. It is in the midst of this world in transition, and with his camera, that he accidentally seems to penetrate the surface of reality.

In a near-deserted park one morning, Thomas comes upon a young woman cavorting with what appears to be her older, male lover. With camera in hand, he pursues them voyeuristically, taking numerous shots, looking to capture something real and unbidden, before he is spotted by the couple. Immediately afterwards, and despite the young woman's desperate attempt to have him hand over the film from his camera, he thinks he has nothing more than some photographs of a peaceful scene to set against the implied brutality of the rest of the images that will make up his book. But as he begins to look more closely at a series of prints in his studio later on in the day, the behaviour of this man and woman, snapped in a moment of apparent innocence, becomes more compelling. It is clear that there was more going on in front of his eyes than he actually saw, or was able to recall (much as what we consciously try to remember becomes difficult to picture in the mind at a later time). Intrigued by the first enigmatic prints, Thomas begins to hone in on a much larger mystery contained in the glance that the young woman (played by Vanessa Redgrave) shoots into some dark bushes behind her lover. This begins a long and well-known section of the movie, portraying the photographer as detective of a suddenly thickened reality, now full of phenomena that only slowly come to light, but which have accidently been revealed by the camera. In working through a succession of enlargements of one small section of an image, he begins to plumb the depths of the Benjaminian optical unconscious.

What we the viewers see as the darkness in the bushes is gradually peeled away to reveal the presence of a deeper reality we might imagine to be forever hidden from the naked eye. Thus, all at once, the enlargements (the 'blow-ups' of the title) offer both more clarity and a greater mystery; what took place that morning and what might be remembered is held in suspense. As a worried Thomas stands in deadly silence before this evidence, looking at what is unmistakably a figure lurking in the bushes, we know that he is experiencing a stomach-churning moment as he tries to reconcile his memory of the events of the morning with what his photographs now reveal. He turns from the enlargements – which are now plastered all over the walls of his studio – bathed in perspiration.

Through a number of other films, Antonioni became known for his interest in the nature of reality. His subject, indeed, often seemed to be reality itself, and how cinema might explore our visual knowledge of it.[67] His work showed a fascination in particular with what at the time was the well-known existentialist concern with how to find meaning in a world that seemed to be increasingly complex. This 'search for meaning', William Pamerleau notes (echoing Benjamin's view of the decline of collective memory), was 'an issue precisely because modern forms of life [had] undermined traditional sources of meaning'.[68] As a modern prosthesis that arguably eclipses almost any other technology for externalizing memory, the camera – which Baudelaire had notably regarded ambivalently, with 'horror and fascination' – possessed magic. But at the same time it was an apparatus for disenchanting the world, due to the fact that it might penetrate into a reality that was better left undisturbed.[69] 'If once it be allowed to impinge on the sphere of the intangible and the imaginary,' Baudelaire wrote, 'then woe betide us.'[70]

Thomas (David Hemmings) probes the optical unconscious in Michelangelo Antonioni's *Blow-Up* (1966). Photographic enlargements, or blow-ups, gradually reveal reality to have a 'depth' that escapes the naked eye but which the camera preserves and the development of film brings to light.

What *Blow-Up* presents us with is the uncomfortable realization that when something seems to be there – as in a photograph or on film – it may produce something quite the opposite of our everyday expectations, which is to reduce what is fleeting and transient into the form of fact. David Alan Mellor, in a masterful exploration of the metaphysical conundrums of this film, suggests that the director was likely influenced by another famous image, Mary Moorman's Polaroid of the assassination of John F. Kennedy in Dallas, Texas, in 1963. It presented a significant 'real-world' forerunner of the fictional concerns of *Blow-Up*. Shot from the opposite side of the road to Abraham Zapruder's better-known home movie of that event, the Polaroid has in its background the infamous grassy knoll where, it was said, a second assassin fired on the Kennedy motorcade. People have wondered for almost 50 years if one of the shapes behind the fence on the grassy knoll, as seen in this image, is a gunman (as some have said on the evidence of enlargements of the image) or simply something more innocuous, literally blown out of proportion by unverifiable association, such a milk bottle caught atop the fence, glinting in the sunshine.

In the end, the lack of certainty merely adds to the puzzle that the most well-known evidence, Zapruder's film, presents to public memory: no matter how often the event could be re-run in the form of the home movie, it could never be more than the ghost of an elusive moment that continues to be the source of disputes to this day. What this short film does do, however, is reinforce the fact that unconscious optics offer a sense of a depthless reality. Perhaps the technology complicates memory as often as not, making reality or the past strange, as much as it offers the recognition of the familiar. As Siegfried Zielinski has argued, it was because the moving image advanced beyond the two-dimensional limitations of the still photograph that it offered the possibility that 'the arrow of time of an event or process could be reversed', with the consequence that 'stretches of time that had become visual information' could be manipulated – by slowing down, zooming in, running backwards – to reveal what the naked eye could never take in.[71]

But it would be strange to end here on a pessimistic note. Photography presents the *possibility* of a record of events, a trace more substantial than the pictures that premoderns presumed to be projected into the back, the interior, of our heads; and, as such, a reality-shifting archive that might accord with an idea of memory as precisely the preservation of traces. As Walter Benjamin would have put it, the Zapruder film represents – as film in general does – the explosion of reality through 'the dynamite of the tenth of a second' (the length of a film frame). It offers to posterity 'an immense and unexpected field of action . . . with the close-up, space expands; with slow motion, movement is extended'.[72]

Sound, Voice, Writing

The surfeit of reality – which we see in the remains, fragments and traces that mass, almost in defiance of time – is emblematic of a temporality that seems more than ever to be defined by 'everyday-ness' and novelty. The development of our archival culture, according to Pierre Nora, accelerates the pace at which we seem to need to preserve everything around us. If this at times seems to herald a new kind of neurosis, it is merely the intensification of a problem that had earlier confronted the seeker of knowledge who went in search of the undiscovered and novel.

A reality conceived only – or merely – in terms of the everyday that might slip away forever was memorably caught in a diary entry by Dr Johnson during a trip to the Scottish Highlands, when he lamented the lack of ink and paper to make a record of the new world he was encountering for the first time. The story, Mary Poovey writes, is not simply presented as a failure of foresight on Johnson's part, but also as 'a trope for a more endemic impediment to epistemological certainty: the failure of memory'.[73] Johnson's remarks on the matter anticipates our own anxieties about a disappearing world, or a world that memory might never take hold of:

> An observer deeply impressed by any remarkable spectacle, does not suppose, that the traces will soon vanish from his mind, and having commonly no great convenience for writ-ing, defers the description to a time of more leisure, and better accommodation. He who has not made the experiment, or who is not accustomed to require rigorous accuracy from

himself, will scarcely believe how much a few hours take from certainty of knowledge, and distinctness of imagery; how the succession of objects will be broken, how separate parts will be confused, and how many particular features and discriminations will be compressed and conglobated into one gross and general idea.[74]

The surfeit – the 'too-muchness' – of the reality thus encountered is produced, in part, by the consciousness that is alert to the particularity of experience; the more minutely it is perceived, the greater the awareness of how much organic memory lacks the ability to store, recall and transmit the details of experience. In a broader sense it defines a cultural life that is today fuelled by the vestiges of what memory – aided by technologies such as the writing aids whose lack Johnson lamented – has preserved as the record of a time, a person, an experience and so on. Archival media technology thrives on the incompleteness of what it records, and becomes all the more evocative for it. A photograph or a pop song, to cite two common examples where the everyday can slip into another temporality, may possess a power far in excess of the modest intentions of its creator, if only because as a fragment it may be freed from the weight of history, thus possessing 'involuntary memories'.[75]

The pre-eminent thinker of the fragmentary nature of modern life is Walter Benjamin, for whom the recuperation of traces and fragments held not only a significant clue to the nature of memory in modernity, but also – in his later writings in particular – the possibility of a greater political awakening or 'remembrance'.[76] For Benjamin, the present was filled with the past, and often in ways that were perhaps not readily acknowledged. 'Doesn't a breath of the air that pervaded earlier days', he once asked, 'caress us?'[77] In many ways the remarkable achievements of media technologies in arresting and preserving the intangible is illustrated by the ways in which sound – ambient sounds, the sound of voices or melodies that evoke the personal – has been written into the archive of cultural memory since the invention of the phonograph.

Sound, as Emily Thompson writes, has 'the mysterious ability to melt into air'; it seems, according to the media philosopher Friedrich

Kittler, to constitute a strange kind of 'weightless matter'.[78] Bridging the realms of the material and the immaterial, the auditory world exists at the intersections of time, space and body. But, through the various technological mediations that carry it into the real of memory, it has had a marked effect at different times on each of these experiential categories – one that is directly related to the ways in which sound is inscribed and stored.

Capturing something as elusive as sound – whether the source is a human voice, music or something more ambient – shares much with other media technologies of storage and transmission. If photography gives us an artificial and super-powerful prosthetic eye, or memory, phonography equally expands the sense of hearing as it relates to consciousness and memory. It creates fragments and abstractions which are snatched from the flow of time. In permitting us to capture or save some aspect of the world we experience through the ears – sensing in terms of recognizable sounds – phonography strangely unmakes the world; it 'destroys sound's ephemeral qualities'.[79]

Thomas Edison and
his phonograph,
c. 1877.

Thus it is useful to remember, as Kittler noted, that audio recording technologies are essentially writing machines, or devices for creating a double or virtual sense of the real, and this has a great power to displace presence.[80] As such, the act of phonographic inscription (or today, sound recording on your smartphone) ultimately permits numerous ghostly traces to become part of how we then perceive ourselves and the world around us. But as a tool that augments our sense of the world, the machine that preserves the trace of sound 'relieves people of their memories', Kittler argued, and brings to bear, in its archive, 'a linguistic hodgepodge' that makes its products more than mere writing.[81]

What is termed the 'post-phonographic' experience – one in which the auditory realm is no longer ephemeral and rooted in the temporal experience of place – is one we take for granted. As recently as the Renaissance, the absence of writing in its various forms ensured that the communication of information, knowledge and experience was by modern standards highly dependent on human memory, and still relied on rhetorical skills, whose results – the outcome of 'inner gymnastics, [and] invisible labours of concentration' – may seem strange to us today, but nonetheless are useful in offering a stark contrast to our contemporary reliance on media of memory.[82] Originating in ancient Greece, this so-called 'artificial memory' took on particular forms in the Middle Ages and Renaissance, as detailed in Frances Yates's book *The Art of Memory* (1966). It was through the theory and practice of rhetoric that this art of memory (as it had came to be called in the Renaissance) had 'travelled down through the European tradition in which it was never forgotten, or not forgotten until comparatively modern times'.[83] As a mnemonic device, it was an art that worked by associating those things that had to be remembered with mental images of striking or unusual places. 'The first step', Yates wrote, 'was to imprint on the memory a series of loci or places', with which certain facts or knowledge to be recalled some time later are then associated; thus an orator moves imaginatively 'through his memory building whilst he is making his speech, drawing from the memorized places the images he has placed on them'.[84]

Quintilian, a first-century Roman orator and teacher of rhetoric who provides one of only several sources on the art of memory, made special note of how the key to a good memory was recognizing the foundational role of experience, and more particularly how the experience of place nurtures memory. 'When we return to a certain place after an interval, we not only recognize it but remember what we did there.'[85] And so it was necessary for students of the art of memory to

> learn sites (*loca*) which are as extensive as possible, and are marked by a variety of objects, perhaps a large house divided into many separate areas. They carefully fix in their mind everything there which is noticeable, so that their thoughts can run over all the parts of it without hesitation or delay. The first task is to make sure that it all comes to mind without any hold-up . . . The next stage is to mark what they have written or are mentally preparing with some sign which will jog their memory.[86]

This 'architectural mnemonic', as Mary Carruthers terms it, extended to much more elaborate practices than those outlined by Quintilian; it is the source of 'modern puzzlement' in the face of what was often an 'apparently cumbersome and odd procedure'.[87]

In providing the means to more permanently inscribe in a form that demanded less of the individual, writing – extending to the printing press, the typewriter and so on – had always promised a painless repetition (by contrast with the labours of the *ars memoria*) that multiplied and made accessible what might once have been uniquely felt, thus overcoming the time-intensive art of transmitting knowledge and information that was mainly characterized by orality.

As well as technology's seemingly autonomous development – once set in motion, it seems driven to ever-greater refinements – the archaic or traditional forms of storing and transmitting knowledge retained such a small world of experience, and were no longer suited to a fast-changing modernity that was, by contrast, continually *expanding* the world of possible experience.

One of a number of texts in which he draws a contrast between the arts of collective memory and the emerging modern media, Walter Benjamin's essay 'The Storyteller' (1936) understands the forms of mass-produced writing (such as the novel and the newspaper) as evidence of a decline in the kind of experience that is deeply rooted in place and presence. As Benjamin noted, it was the storyteller who gave life to tradition, and thus to the past, which, in an important sense, linked storytelling with mortality. The 'communicability of experience' that had once been born of the sustained efforts of memory, Benjamin suggested, gave authority to the 'natural history' that stories could not help but express.[88] Benjamin's use of the term 'natural history' refers to a human continuity with the realm of the dead (conceived of as generations of ancestors) that was brought to life through representations of the past. This idea also signals a recognition that human progress, no matter how much it tries, can never ultimately escape a temporality we associate with nature, and with cycles of generation and decay. Thus, by contrast with traditional forms of communication, as illustrated in the old, wise figure of the storyteller, modern media technologies signal the possibility of eluding the grip of death. But this is at the expense of authentic memory, which in modern society would be remade through a host of technologies that sever our connection to the past, thus enabling us to be thrust ever more certainly into the maelstrom of a continually moving present.

Benjamin's writings are perhaps exemplary in exploring the association between media, the materiality of temporal existence and memory to suggest that those objects and phenomena that seemed to capture time (obsolete products, the world of the kitsch and the banal, and so on) do not just provide simple aids to memory. What interested him rather more were the phantasmagorical dimensions of the material past as it was carried into the present. In this sense, the materialization of sound and music – its existence on wax cylinders, vinyl records, tape and other hard formats – seems to make available an auditory realm that necessarily develops on the basis of a subjective consciousness of sound, and a receptivity to it that has also always been pursued as a passion; that is to say, as a phenomenon that engages memory and emotion. These material traces of the auditory world take us into a 'soundscape' which, as Emily Thompson argues, depends on a human relation to space; it is both 'a physical environment and way of perceiving that environment'.[89] The historical development of audio technology has not only altered the soundscape, but also our access to and expectations of it. Thus each new advance in sound media modifies the human relationship to a changing sound-scape that is driven by the very material form of sound. It is interesting to note that discerning consumers of audio technologies, for instance, tended to seek out an increasingly abstract aural stimulation that was channelled in the direction of the isolated listener. Abstracted from time and place, the sounds of the phonographic world became increasingly 'clear and focused', Thompson suggests, 'with little opportunity to reflect and reverberate off the surfaces of the room in which it was generated', as would be the case where headphones were used to block out the environmental sounds that actually located the listener in place.[90]

The apparent artificiality of what Michel Serres calls the polychronic, multitemporal nature of how we live through objects and technologies – drawing simultaneously on 'the obsolete, the contemporary, and the futuristic' – reflects the efficacy of these fragments of sound, and what they do to consciousness and memory.[91] When Benjamin laments the demise of storytelling it is in the service of an attempt to remember a world in which experience had not yet been fragmented; not yet wrenched from an immemorial tradition that offered wisdom rather than information, and comfort rather than alienation. The soundscape of such a world is evoked to great effect in Alain Corbin's account of the changes modern life enforced upon the soundscape of rural France, *Village Bells*. Here Corbin gives a sense of a world approaching modernity, and through the details of the spatio-temporal upheavals that it would unleash we see the hitherto unremarkable history of sound and its very centrality to collective life and memory. The simple fact was that the village bells that the authorities – who were keen on breaking the hold of the past – had set upon removing marked both spatial and human boundaries. The sounds that issued from these bells constituted – as much as landscape, dwelling places and so on – the possibility of an experience of something like home.

'The crucial functions of the bell tower', Corbin noted, were to 'raise the alarm and ensure the preservation of the community'.

It was important to ensure that no part of that territory remained obdurately deaf to public announcements, alarms, or commands, and that there were no fragments of isolated space in which the auditory identity was ill-defined and threatened to impede rapid assembly.[92]

This was a soundscape, in other words, caught within the rhythms of a world bound by the unity of experience, sentiment and place: what was heard depended on – indeed, could not be separated from – one's physical proximity to the actual content of experience, its relation to real and specific people, objects and phenomena. Yet for all that, such a soundscape essentially bound the individual within a collective life that was defined by place; the premodern world in this sense is arguably defined not merely by place but importantly also by time and duration. In other words, sound is there, it exists, and then it is gone. Its repetitions in everyday life reflect the largely unchanging nature of life and remain always rooted in temporal presence.

When the means to record and preserve sound arrived in the nineteenth century into a world that had previously been defined as a soundscape by temporal duration and presence, it did so through artefacts that released the grip of the old reality. No longer, in an experiential sense and in terms of consciousness, was hearing rooted to place. Once this sense of the world in its 'wholeness' is broken, experience finds itself amid the remnants of time and memory: isolated sounds – a voice, or a musical performance never witnessed at first hand – that belong somewhere else. The effect of the phonograph to those first exposed to it was more dramatic than we can easily comprehend today, precisely because it might have seemed like some kind of voodoo art that allowed its early adepts to 'toy with the present, undo origin, and realign memory' in ways that were entirely foreign to human experience up to that point in time.[93]

The surfeit of reality produced by such means nonetheless merely pushes the reality-warping potential of media technologies into a particular aspect of sensory experience, namely hearing. The implications of memory externalized in *written* form reaches back to the earliest philosophical reflections on what it meant to be human. A distrust of writing, in fact, arguably emerges along with writing itself. The most renowned discussion of the peculiar dangers of writing for memory is to be found in Plato's *Phaedrus*, in which Socrates recounts a myth centred on the inventor of writing, Theuth, who attempted to convince the king of Egypt that this so-called 'potion for memory and intelligence' should be learned throughout the land for the general improvement of the people. The king, though, thinks otherwise:

> You are most ingenious, Theuth. [But] the loyalty you feel to writing, as its originator, has just led you to tell me the opposite of its true effect. It will atrophy people's memories. Trust in writing will make them remember things by relying on marks made by others, from outside themselves, not on their own inner resources, and so writing will make the things they have learnt disappear from their minds. Your invention is a potion for jogging the memory, not for remembering.[94]

In addition to this difficulty – that externalizing memory leads to an easily attained but depthless kind of 'intelligence' – more recently there has been much written exploring the implied narcosis of this writing as described by Socrates. It is one of the subjects of Jacques Derrida's well-known essay 'Plato's Pharmacy', in which his attention is particularly drawn to the description of writing as a *pharmakon* (in the translation above quoted it is rendered as 'potion', and elsewhere as 'charm'). Derrida's aim was to explore more fully the implication that writing is a kind of drug that might lead us astray. As such, whatever experience, knowledge, learning and so on is gained through it, it nevertheless can only disturb the relation a person has with place. It is by virtue of this that it could be thought to deviate from the path of real wisdom:

> Operating through seduction, the *pharmakon* makes one stray from one's general, natural, habitual paths and laws. Here, it takes Socrates out of his proper place and off his customary track. The latter had always kept him inside the city. The leaves [that is, pages] of writing act as a *pharmakon* to push or attract out of the city the one who never wanted to get out, even at the end, to escape the hemlock. They take him out of himself and draw him onto a path that is properly an *exodus*.[95]

Thus, Derrida goes on to suggest, Socrates prostrates himself before the reader of one of these written speeches, almost like a visitor to a nineteenth-century opium den awaiting his elixir. This is something that Socrates – who, we learn, never leaves his home town because there is nothing to be learned beyond contact with real people – then invites and accepts in full knowledge of its dangers. He admits of what would not be possible if the speech were merely spoken; that in its written form it possesses, as Derrida says, a kind of narcotic quality in that it promises a repetition of pleasure that speech itself cannot guarantee. It is an experience that is destructive of the conditions of reality, if not the *placeness* of real experience and real memory. 'A spoken speech . . . a speech proffered *in the present, in the presence* of Socrates, would not have had the same effect', Derrida says:

> Only the *logoi en bibliois*, only words that are deferred, reserved, enveloped, rolled up, words that force one to wait for them in the form and under cover of a solid object, letting themselves be desired for the space of a walk, only hidden letters can thus get Socrates moving. If a speech could be purely present, unveiled, naked, offered up in person in its truth, without the detours of a signifier foreign to it, if at the limit an undeferred *logos* were possible, it would not seduce anyone. It would not draw Socrates, as if under the effects of a *pharmakon*, out of his way.[96]

The difficulty from the outset, therefore, has been that externalizing in the form of a medium something which would otherwise require to be memorized – the speeches of others, in this case – would come to institute the 'mnemotechnical auxiliary' of a bad, inauthentic memory.[97]

The medium itself, any such medium – and it is no less true today – revolves around a dialectic of remembering and forgetting. If, for Plato (through Socrates), this held out the possibility of delivering up a world in which 'the dead and rigid knowledge shut up in *biblia*, [in] piles of histories, nomenclatures, recipes and formulas learned by heart' took precedence over 'living knowledge', it would be a victory, Derrida remarked, 'for whatever works in an occult manner ... governed by the laws of magic', rather than by the authentic experience of the face-to-face encounter with wisdom that the Socratic dialectic promised.[98]

Yet those fears come to be accommodated in a culture that is defined, in one way or another, through an 'epistemology of writing as a medium able to transcend time as well as space'.[99] This is especially true of the arts of knowledge, of learning as it has developed since the Renaissance, if not before, and which now seems far removed from the Socratic ideal. 'We are shamans at heart', Aleida Assmann says,

> recreating a continuous conversation with ancestral voices and the spirits of the past. We not only work with media in the technical sense, literary texts and theatrical performances, for instance, but we also are media in the occult sense of establishing contact with a transcendent world for collective benefit.[100]

But such is the tension between remembering and forgetting that is always inherent in mediated experience: to record or inscribe is to preserve time and experience, but also, in a sense, to forget in the very act of 'outsourcing' memory.

What complicates phonography's relation to time and memory further is that like the camera, the phonograph (and, we read here, its successors) 'seemed to inscribe or "capture" sound indiscriminately, capaciously – anything from noise to music – without regard to speaker or source'.[101] Think of the environmental sounds of the cinema foley, which adds depth and richness (and perhaps artifice) to the visual counterparts of the soundtrack; think, too, of the musical nuance that is amplified through the preserved trace, and so on. Any such sound recording technology is therefore a machine that provides access to what Benjamin, in relation to photography, described as the 'optical unconscious'; that is to say, it creates an auditory unconscious.[102] Or, again, media technologies don't just mediate: they double, replicate and expand the world of possible experience. In other words, what the machine unintentionally identifies is a world that possibly comes to awareness independently of any human interest in it, let alone any intention to capture or make something of it. It is a phenomenon that leads Friedrich Kittler, in his discussion of modern technologies of transmission and storage, to suggest that by a kind of back-to-front analogy, the Freudian unconscious – with its phantasms and unwelcome memories, lapsing into an apparently primitive pre-history of the self – is defined by a 'media logic'.[103] That is, it gives form to a storehouse of experiences that are free-floating.

Where Freud's unconscious points to a kind of mysterious undergrowth in a subject's past, Benjamin's notion posits modern media technology – the camera, printing – as a set of devices that gives material reality to the invisible and imperceptible; reality is no longer merely what the subject experiences through the senses, but reveals itself as a 'constellation' within which the human might be found. As the artist Gerhard Richter writes, it was 'the level of inscription, specifically the ability of the apparatus . . . to register aspects of a material reality' that demonstrated for Benjamin that the camera, with its access to phenomena that pass us by, would become in the future – like media in general – the source of our consciousness.[104]

Much the same applies to the auditory unconscious. As the sound artist David Toop writes in *Haunted Weather*, even those silences that constitute our many social rituals are no longer just silence once materialized as recorded sound. To listen to historical recordings of the minute's silence of long-past Armistice Day ceremonies, Toop notes, reveals that what is thought of an absence, 'the withdrawal of noise (in all its senses) is replaced by a louder phenomenon', derived from 'a focusing of attention'.[105] In these 'silences' we hear the noise of passing time. Thus the material existence of the past ensures it can 'return virtually any sound back again and again into the sensorium and into the historical register'.[106] When EMI Records, for instance, released new versions of The Beatles recordings on compact disc in the 1980s, the clarity of cleaned-up ('remastered') recordings – rather like the act of wiping clean the dirt on the surface of an Old Master – revealed previously unnoticed details, including, to the amusement of many, the sound of Ringo Starr's kick drum pedal, which now squeaked its way into the historical register. It may even have served to remind the drummer of something he had no prior memory of.

For all its revelations, this was still implicit in what phonographic technology had always promised: the reproduction of sounds that might otherwise have been lost to time. As the material form of a kind of memory, it had, for over half a century, nonetheless 'produced objects that could be consumed only in their manufactured form'.[107] It was not until the development of magnetic tape in the late 1930s and its increasing use in the 1940s and '50s that sound became *material* in a plastic sense – that is to say, like clay or paint – thereby advancing its artistic potential. Once this had occurred, the potential for sound to yet again remake consciousness and memory became clear.

Bush of Ghosts

We might say that media remake human memory as a kind of cultural kaleidoscope. The potential to go from experiencing displaced time – a *real* that is absent – in recorded sound, to the polychromic auditory world introduced by the medium of magnetic tape, takes the materiality of sound yet further into 'reverie, myth, and fantasies of cosmic journeys'.[108] It had the potential to produce a soundscape characterized by what Benjamin termed 'dialectical images'.[109]

Magnetic tape, unlike the hard format of early recordable sound media, was characterized by its pliability. It afforded greater artistic potential simply because it could be cut, spliced, looped and doubled, giving it the potential to produce 'powerful and paradoxical techno-conceptual' syntheses, whose effects on the experience of time and place gained additional impact from means of processing that engaged 'repetition and mutation, presence and delay'.[110]

Early experiments in these methods were made in France during the late 1940s and '50s, when Pierre Schaeffer developed a technique that became known as *musique concrète*.[111] Alongside others involved in the Groupe de Recherche de Musique Concrète (established within Radiodiffusion-Télévision Française in 1951), he employed the new magnetic tape technology to 'harness sound's intrinsic ambiguity or malleability'. This development would produce a new kind of music, or sound art, that had little to do with traditional notions of composition or performance. Instead it 'pulled' phenomena out of the atmosphere, allowing artists to play upon 'the technological mechanics, physics and inherent nuance of sounds as revealed through the properties of phonograph records, magnetic tape and the recording studio.[112] The object of *musique concrète* was the real environment of sound, and in practice it sought to utilize fragments of 'noise' (or non-musical sounds) to create an electroacoustic equivalent of collage in visual media. For visual artists, the goal of collage was similarly to mine the detritus of everyday life for its aesthetic potential. Kurt Schwitters, for instance, would compose his collages using the fragments of daily life, which might include 'used tram tickets, cloakroom tokens, beer mats, scraps of newspaper, candy wrappers, splinters of glass and metal, wood-shavings, chickenwire, bits of discarded string' and so on.[113] As Schaeffer recalled, *musique concrète*'s own 'real' consisted of such phenomena as 'thunderstorms, steam-engines, waterfalls, [and] steel foundries', which were recorded and then 'manipulated to form sound structures'.[114]

Unlike the contemporaneous experiments with sound being produced in Germany by members of the movement that went by the name of Elektronische Musik, bricolage was more important than composition in *musique concrète*; plundering the auditory unconscious a more commonly used method than synthesizing sounds that a lis-tener could not associate with the real, lived environment.[115] This possibility of recognition gave it an added force, introducing the listener to sounds that seemed familiar, but were rendered strange. Recorded sound's inherent capacity for warping time, space and memory, however, was particularly marked when it came to the use of the human voice in such audio collages.

In the early tape works of the American composer Steve Reich (most notably two pieces from the mid-1960s, 'Come Out' and 'It's Gonna Rain'), the human voice was made to 'mutate and transform kaleidoscopically' under the action of machine agency, slipping in and out of sync, 'to capture poignant, contradictory moments in the sonic equivalent of what Benjamin referred to as "the dialectical image"'.[116]

In Benjamin's work, as Ben Highmore observes, 'everyday life registers the process of modernization as an incessant accumulation of debris'.[117] And it was through the medium of debris, raised to the level of the aesthetic, that he thought we might be awakened from the dreamworld of modernity's perpetual present. The possibility of a new consciousness of time and progress lay behind his own Arcades

The French composer Pierre Schaeffer in 1961.

Project, which itself piled up fragments (quotations, observations and aphorisms) in a kind of literary montage inspired by the ideas of Surrealism. Benjamin thought that such fragments, when placed in the right combinations and juxtapositions, would allow the dead world of modernity past to come into its own.[118]

The use of the term 'dialectical image' should not be taken to refer simply to 'images' in a visual or photographic sense. Rather, the word 'image' here refers to something closer to *thought-image* – perhaps a kind of dreamlike synthesis or, as Benjamin observed, 'the realization of dream elements in the course of waking up is the canon of dialectics'. The dialectical image thus fuses time, experience and memory to suggest new possibilities, or an otherwise concealed reality in which things put on 'their true – surrealist – face'.[119]

To relate this to technologies that permit the preservation of sound is to bring us some way from a means of inscribing sound that offered a simple copy of a chunk of reality. It takes us more fully into the kind of occult presence that seemed to lurk within Plato's fear that writing displaced experience, and in particular the directness of the Socratic dialectic as a route to truth. Dialectics in Benjamin's work, by contrast, drew on a different source to find a new truth in a post-media reality – not the directly human, but rather the human in its fragmented and mediated forms. Brian Eno and David Byrne's album of 1981, *My Life in the Bush of Ghosts*, is one remarkable example of how the preserved sound of a human voice, in one sense a fragment of the past, can be thrown into new and revealing combinations, aided by the kind of sensibility that impelled Shaeffer's development of *musique concrète*. Described at one stage as a kind of 'garbage disco' because it was composed of a variety of found sounds, this album was a collection of audio collages that took the form of something not far removed from popular song. Following the tradition of *musique concrète*, everyday objects found lying close at hand – cardboard boxes, ashtrays and tins, and the sounds that could be extracted from them – were used in place of traditional musical instruments. Building on the example of Steve Reich's early tape works, Eno and Byrne made the voice central to this project: in one 'song', for instance, we hear a radio evangelist; in others, spiritual singers, an apologetic politician and, on one piece, an 'unidentified exorcist'. These voices constitute the ghosts of the album's title.

But, at another level of understanding, we can see yet more ghosts – and not merely those that are the effect of technology's uncanny properties. Imagine, if you will, *Roget's Thesaurus* as the most fantastical and orderly inventory of self and other yet contrived by the human mind in order to come to terms with how experience has thus far been understood and accounted for. Everything, we learn, begins with one fundamental opposition: there is existence and there is non-existence. From there, all language, all understanding, may be derived. To seek further is to see that all the subordinate categories of meaning that language allows us to attach to life and death end up strangely concealing the dependence of these two fundamental opposites beneath an endless elaboration of phenomena – in the language through which we imagine and give sense to reality – that offer the protection of disguise; a cloak of familiarity.

Yet force any of the oppositions that language, in its fondness for contrasts, hides behind into collision and you will find paradoxes, indeterminacy and the unconscious. Soon, you raise to life a world of 'intuition, revelation and inspiration, and of in-between media like air, angels and spirits'.[120]

On one 'level' beneath the fundamental opposition of all that is living and dead in our inventory we find ghosts, or the simulacra of the real. As emanations of 'another place and another time' they return as a kind of counter-memory that lays claim to the present, or at least threatens to catapult us back into some mythic temporality where forces beyond our control dominate, causing – as Vernant said apropos of the voyage to Hades – 'the descent of a living person into the underworld for the purpose of finding out – and seeing – what he wants to know'.[121] If we look at this artefact, *My Life in the Bush of Ghosts*, we might wonder if this had always been the aim of both Eno and Byrne, and what caused them to find each other. Eno's well-known 'oblique strategies' are one obvious example of this desire to be taken over, to be 'possessed', guided by some other force. But we see it all the way through David Byrne's career, too – from his earliest and mostly unknown days as a performance art student at the Rhode Island School of Design, for instance, where he once posed in a photograph as a living map of the United States, eyes blanked out in denial of self; a surface, a medium, on which some other thing could write itself.

The realm of ghosts, of possession and loss, leads us back, inevitably it seems, to myths. Ancient myths especially reveal the dangers of dabbling with the past and disturbing the supposedly dormant or exhausted forces that were likely just lying in some temporary slumber, as if waiting to be roused. In Virgil's *Georgics* the ghosts or 'shades' from the underworld are conjured up, of course, by the music of Orpheus, to be found amid the leaves of a bush:

> But, by his song aroused from Hell's nethermost basements,
> Flocked out the flimsy shades (ghosts), the phantoms lost to light,
> In number like the millions of birds that hide in the leaves.[122]

Once again the image of the bush, like the bushes Thomas probes in Antonioni's *Blow-Up*, stand for a depth we might equate with an unconscious; with a human presence not known and, as such, strange. In *My Life in the Bush of Ghosts*, Eno and Byrne raise to the forefront of consciousness that which might otherwise vanish, or at least remain hidden. They entertain possession by something that might move them, pull them back into a time and place where self was unimportant, as if they were anonymous scribes or mediums through which the dead come to take possession of the living. It was an album significant in advancing the aesthetics of everyday life and its fragments into a popular music still hamstrung by notions of authenticity, and which tended to see artistic merit in self-expression, or the artistic voice (understood in the most unremarkable of ways). Importantly, its intention was to allow its creators the possibilities of forgetting themselves and disappearing into the auditory unconscious – the metaphorical 'bush of ghosts' – to make, Byrne later remarked, 'a series of recordings based on an imaginary culture' that might have 'a Borges-like quality'.[123]

Against the claims of an aesthetics of authenticity, *My Life in the Bush of Ghosts* therefore worked by effacing the voice and throwing discrete fragments against a musical backdrop to which they did not seem to belong. Its revelation seemed to be that technology renders our world into fragments – and, moreover, it *fragments* selves – and that this was really how we should now listen to it, and hear its weird, warped music. What Eno and Byrne recognized, as Benjamin did in his way, was that their creative intentions should be allowed to give way to an unconscious. What they might have conceived of on the basis of experience, or self-knowledge, counted less than what might be found in the 'bush of ghosts'. That this expression – borrowed from the title of a novel by Amos Tutuola – would become the title for this project was interesting in itself. It stood as an apt metaphor for the limitless possibilities of an auditory world opened up by tape recording technology. Everything, *My Life in the Bush of Ghosts* suggests, is part of a chain of chance that gathers in the proximate, the tangential, the contingent – but which, as Michel Serres said in another respect, becomes a 'chain that steadies the phenomenal'.[124] That locates experience in 'liquid history and the ages of the waters':

Here then is the chain: white sea or white plain, background noise, surge, fluctuation of the surge, bifurcation, repetition, rhythm or cadence, vortex. The great turbulence is constituted, it fades away, it breaks. And disappears as it came.

This chain is breaking, it is breaking at every point, it may always break, its characteristic is to snap. It is fragile, unstable . . .

It must be an element of the drives and pulls of nature, it is a bit of life's secret, a series of sudden and risky leaps of thought that can invent, throw itself into the noise, support itself in redundancy, a long piece of melody, sometimes rhythmic, in tempo as it were, sometimes letting go, as by a free end, some proposition that is aperiodical but right.

It is a little bit of the secret thrust of our awakenings, and the timid and green advance of the new. Look at it: it is the dance of time, which is dormant in our habitual behavior.[125]

Sound, music and voice possess us and take us to places we would never have imagined could be reached. Eno and Byrne may have conceived of their work as the means to conjure into existence a reality that might have emerged from a fantastical Borges story, but what their album enacted equally was akin to a Benjaminian understanding of memory as the 'ability to interpolate endlessly in what has been'.[126] They did this precisely by catching and preserving moments that otherwise would have passed according to the laws of ephemerality – here today, gone later today – and which was particularly the case with the 'weightless matter' of radio broadcasts that quite often became their source material.

The Sound in Your Head

The artists who experimented with the spatial qualities of sound in order to manipulate and create a new and synthetic auditory world were also predominantly in search of a means to escape the artistic 'I', which we might equally regard as a kind of learned memory of their own habits and dispositions. This was all to engage with an 'auditory unconscious', hitherto unremarked on aside from the awareness of sound's ephemerality, which had been revealed through the earliest sound recordings. Yet with respect to how their works were received and consumed, they nonetheless presented a subjectivity that aimed to connect with that of a listener. Of their traces, ghostly emanations of another time and place, in other words, they made objects – works of art, collages of sound that remade our understanding of music. But what happens when we are awash in the fragments ourselves, and without the mediation of the artistic object?

As a result of the most recent developments in these technologies that capture and transmit a sound world, the subjectivity of the artist – of Brian Eno and David Byrne, for instance – is no longer necessarily the subjectivity of the listener or consumer. Consumers of recorded music, in particular, can, and now do, mash-up their own world of sound.

Today, sound objects, seemingly dematerialized, merge with technological hardware (computers, mobile devices) in a more perfect kind of synchronicity than ever before to give birth to a way of being that is defined less by old ideas of experience as a kind of temporal duration than it is by sensory immersion or immediacy. As Fredric Jameson has argued, the apparatus of new media and communications technology appears in our lives increasingly as a form of 'the promotion and transfiguration of the synchronic'; as the means for being in a continuous temporal present, rather than the 'being-in-time' of experience.[127] The smartphone in your pocket or your hand allows you to 'surf' what Harvie Ferguson calls the 'selfless non-identity' of a present in which *feeling* and *mood* become the sensual counterpart to the fragmentation of life.[128] This is one form of the phenomenological reduction to the present which in turn ends up grounded in the sensations of the body. If it *feels* good that is what matters, and it is by definition good, or 'meaningful'.[129] And it is in feeling – in the body, in other words – that a sound world that was once ephemeral now finds itself; it is your personal world of sound, and it offers the means, like so many media, to switch realities.

What, though, of the material culture that sustains the immersed body? The potential offered by the post-phonographic auditory world was that the machine and the material artefact, the turntable and the disc, presented, or enhanced, 'the structuring of perceptual experience in terms of a solitary rather than a collective subject',[130] while that tendency towards the isolation of experience – Benjamin's fear with regard to writing replacing the arts of transmission more associated with a world of collective memory – has continued to gather momentum. Thus the sound *in your head* will now often be totally unrelated to place. Today 'the majority of westerners possess the technology to create their own private mobile auditory world wherever they go'.[131] The kind of immersion in the now that this permits has now given rise to a new malady that afflicts memory and attention: 'iPod oblivion', an unwitting confusion of sense that arises from the disjunction between sound world and physical world that seems to afflict urban dwellers who should know better, caught – as they often are – wandering aimlessly into the passage of oncoming buses and delivery vans.[132]

The transfiguration of sound into something akin to a bodily sensation, remote-controlled from your own unique handheld device, goes together with the further distancing of the old auditory world; it's a depth of field phenomenon in which the artificial soundscape, served up by the capacious potential of digital memory, draws our attention – just as the real melts into a blur of indistinct, silent movement, offering a strange disconnected kind of animation to what you might naturally hear at such times. But beyond the simple facts of how much this relies on the staggering expansion of data (or memory) storage – its capacity grows ever larger as its physical form shrinks – it makes it possible to access vast virtual libraries of audio content via the fabled 'Celestial Jukebox' or 'networked library of all the music ever recorded', which will increasingly be 'available instantly, anywhere, anytime'.[133] The idea of playing an album from beginning to end in the sequence intended by a recording artist is therefore 'thrown out in favour of allowing machines to choose songs at random, which then often leads to unexpected, magical juxtapositions of music'.[134]

The theoretical possibility of this plenitude would seem to be one of the clearest indications yet that new media technologies maintain their hold because they can so effectively service the kind of passion that seeks 'the comfort of oblivion'.[135] Indeed, as Jameson suggests, the phenomenological reduction to the present that characterizes much of contemporary life finds its only support in the notion of the eternal – to be out of time, even if we are wedded to the experience of passionate moments, can be nothing else.[136] Alongside the promise of network society – particularly in the positive potential of its new social media – there is nonetheless a technological drive towards the temporal fragmentation of 'experience' as a kind of being-in-the-moment. This both sustains and accelerates the development of the entire ecology of new media, which promises the kind of encounters that are immersive and synchronic, thus heralding an 'end of temporality'.[137] Such an end is found, as Ferguson notes, in a host of 'saturated phenomena' – one instance of which might be the aforementioned Celestial Jukebox – which 'overwhelm the living moment with content . . . and enter memory in the attenuated form of "having taken place" while preserving nothing of the moment itself'.[138] New media technologies enable us to access and orchestrate a continual flow of bits and pieces that may take numerous forms – auditory, visual or textual, and so on – but which produce a flow of sounds, images and thoughts that reconfigure memory and experience.

The transformation of sound from an object of *experience* out there in the world to a mediated rush that nourishes *inner space*, the private and interior, illustrates the lure of forgetting when a continual present offers itself up through a seemingly infinite digital archive. What it suggests is that time and memory are multitemporal conditions of an existence that may easily be bent, dissolved and remade into a fleeting form that suits the purposes of unknown passions.

III

Ecologies

In the future, memory, intellect and imagination will no longer have
need of one another – from elements of our spirit they will become,
if you like – components, members, and independent spirits.

Novalis

Heritage meets myth in the memory of war, and in particular
the memory of the Second World War. It was the time at which
this new phenomenon of a memory, at once existentially displaced
and held in some obscure cultural ether, shifted attention from the
more obvious effects of time's passing – preserving landscape or
threatened buildings as our heritage – into a sphere of what the French
sociologist Emile Durkheim termed the *'conscience collective'*, or
collective conscious. The great benefit of Durkheim's notion is to
acknowledge and remind us that the life of any individual would not
amount to much if one were to remove the culture – the world – that
it is orientated within and towards. But because memory is, in a way,
always concerned with the transmission of something that is absent,
and is not reducible to an empirical reality, this *conscience collective*
expresses the sense of who we are that we do not possess or own.

That was taken to be the means by which the past, in a modernity
essentially cut off from immemorial tradition, was communicated to
the present. In Raphael Samuel's detailed account of the multifaceted
nature of memory as a kind of stage on which we conjure up a post-
historical and post-media sense of the collective, we find an idealistic
nobility in 'the British Way' and a carefully embroidered story about
moral character that came to the fore when 'the country stood alone
against the forces of tyranny and darkness'.[1] This is the language of the
myth and the epic. 'Myths might be the dreams of mankind', David
Adams Leeming suggests, which sees them essentially as a 'means of
escape' driven by 'wishes and fears'. Myths, he adds, might 'serve whole
societies and . . . many societies at once in the same manner'.[2]

Collective Representations

What we might learn from this assertion of the persistence of myth is that in spite of the elevation of Enlightenment ideals to do with the triumph of reason and science, and Western society's long-drawn-out affair with progress and the pursuit of a utopian space that would cleanse us of the past and its mess and error, myth nonetheless lurks all around. It is inescapable for the same reason that the depth psychology of Freud and others gathered so much momentum in the twentieth century: the human condition depends on memory. Memory connects us to myths of origin, if not to a sense of time immemorial, because our very distance from that originary condition demands the creation of a symbolic universe which can give order to the temporal disjunction of an experience that is both cut off from the past and yet aware of it as something seemingly inalienable. We should not be so quick to assume that myth gets left behind just because progress or modernity seems to have triumphed. The mythographer Mircea Eliade, for instance, relates 'primordial' memory to our own, modern, approach to the past, which seems as equally as myth to be caught up in the notion that the past provides an accurate signpost to the future:

> Those . . . who are able to remember their former lives are above all concerned with discovering their own 'history', parcelled out as it is among their countless incarnations. They try to unify these isolated fragments, to make them parts of a single pattern, in order to discover the direction and meaning of their destiny.[3]

Discourses around the character of modernity, especially Baudelairean modernity – which posit a world of contingent relations and ephemeral phenomena – conventionally contrast it with the experience of a premodern or archaic world, in which tradition was the glue that kept everything in its place. Immemorial tradition, a time not touched by memory as we know it, was informed by the habits and repetitions that are congruent with a present that is always given by its place. Thus, for Alain Corbin, the sound of village bells, as we saw, forms part of the atmosphere of a closed world. But in historical terms, from a distanced present, it is a characteristic of that world, an aspect of phenomenal experience that constitutes one element of 'the invisible, the momentary, and the perishable', which marks that kind of lifeworld as it came face to face with the new.[4] To contrast the modern with the archaic or the traditional is to understand premodern temporality as being either 'oriented towards repeating cycles', or to 'the promises of divine eternity'.[5] The consequences of modernity were catastrophic for this world; at once, it 'dashes traditional structures and lifeways to pieces, sweeps away the sacred, undermines immemorial habits and inherited languages'.[6]

As time was quantified, rationalized and made the basis of the new industrial rhythms that fashion life, the new men and women of this modern world lost a sense of the timelessness that was generally characteristic of a more innocent existence lived within a space that we would equate with the idea of home. Rural patterns of labour, set to a rhythm of seasonal and place constraints, for instance, meant that 'men [had] determined their own existence through bouts of intense labour alternated with idleness'.[7] Modernity, hollowed out by unnatural clock time, seems to leave – by contrast – only 'the deep bottomless vegetative time of Being itself, no longer draped and covered with myth or inherited religion'.[8] This is all to say that modern self-consciousness, which transforms memory through its acute sense of loss, lives out a separation of the isolated individual from home – from the immemorial or unchanging; it stakes out its self-awareness first of all in a recognition that the modern world is not the same as the past, and thereafter in its awareness of human finitude.

*

DEVELOPING HIS NOTION of collective conscious in *The Elementary Forms of Religious Life*, Durkheim wrote of the persistence of affective and ritualistic practices in the everyday life of modern societies. These were constituted in habits, practices and occasions which bound individuals together through an idea – a 'self-image' – of possessing a shared past, or at least aspects of a common tradition. He thought that when individuals meet or reconvene – at reunions or other occasional assemblies, for instance – they reach towards sentiments that are essentially religious in their form and function. And so, even when it is avowedly secular, modern society will at important times revolve around 'ceremonies which do not differ from religious ceremonies, either in their object, the results which they produce, or the processes employed to attain these results'.[9]

For Durkheim, the system of beliefs common to such groups constitutes a 'mythology', whose purpose is to preserve, reawaken and enact traditions which are given form in a system of beliefs that can be nothing other than a social 'memory' that is 'a moral system and a cosmology as well as a history':

> So the rite serves and can serve only to sustain the vitality of these beliefs, to keep them from being effaced from memory and, in sum, to revivify the most essential elements of the collective consciousness.[10]

As a founder of the new discipline of sociology in the late nineteenth century, Durkheim held that the mere idea of the modern individual, possessed of a capacity for rational thought, had to suggest that self-hood was 'highly dependent on social existence', particularly 'since individual existence is too fluid and changeable' to engender the kind of routine, stability and habit that might inform a rational orientation to the world.[11]

The most notable expression of the Durkheimian view of the *conscience collective* that would come to be formulated explicitly in the language of memory – and addressing the perceived limits of philosophical abstraction – was found in the works of one of Durkheim's students, Maurice Halbwachs, who developed and elaborated an idea of 'collective memory' that differed in significant ways from the uses of the term by others, such as Walter Benjamin (whose understanding of it was more allusive) and Aby Warburg (whose work developed an idea of social memory).[12] This collective memory consisted of 'a web of intersecting frames of references' – the perspectives of persons whom we might mistakenly think of as individuals; their experiences overlap with others and criss-cross into a sort of invisible and temporary web of relations, which gives us the collective conscious.[13] 'What makes recent memories hang together', Halbwachs insisted,

Korean War Veterans Memorial, Washington, DC. Jan Assmann: 'History turns into myth as soon as it is remembered, narrated, and used, that is, woven into the fabric of the present.'

is that they are part of a totality of thoughts common to a group, the group of people with whom we have a relationship at this moment, or with whom we have had a relation on the preceding day or days.[14]

When Halbwachs argued that there was no such thing as individual memory, he was also taking aim at his near contemporary, Henri Bergson, the author of *Matter and Memory*, whose idea of memory – based as it was on a notion of temporal 'duration' that identified existence in terms of a continuous consciousness – rested on the idea of a realm that was 'interior' and 'incorporeal'.[15] In the preface to the writings published under the title *On Collective Memory*, Halbwachs pondered the question of what exactly might make recollection possible.

Through the example of a story dating from 1731, and recounting the experience of a young girl who had been abandoned and was found wandering far from home in southern France, he began to draw out some of the ideas that would form the basis of his theory of collective memory. In the tale as it was discovered by Halbwachs, the lost child had been said to have 'kept no recollection of her child-hood', yet it seemed that she may have been born 'in the north of Europe, probably among the Eskimos', since she was able to recount having 'twice crossed large distances by sea'.[16] We learn from this tale that she responded emotionally in a way that could only indicate the familiarity of home 'when shown pictures of huts or boats from Eskimo country', as well as other examples of the kinds of sights or images that seem to raise the past once again from the depths of memory.[17]

Through the use of this example, Halbwachs was making a very simple point about how utterly meaningless a concept of memory outside some collective or social framework was. Following Durkheim's notion that the collective requires a 'self-image' of its past as a means of survival, then within the context of modernity representing the supposed overcoming of irrational beliefs, the association of memory with an *individual* consciousness seems to stem from the same motivation as the Cartesian attempt to make personhood solely dependent on the workings of the rational mind – which itself was an attempt to defeat dreams and illusions, or what we otherwise might call myth. It is a move that necessarily treats the collective with suspicion, thus pushing myth – as Durkheim used the term – into those corners of modern life where the last vestiges of the archaic and of tradition may be found. Thus Gianni Vattimo argues that when we talk of myth today it is understood to belong to phenomena that are opposed to the scientific, rational kind of doubting that Descartes proclaimed as his method.

> Unlike scientific thought, myth is not demonstrative or analytic . . . but narrative and fantastic, playing on the emotions with little or no pretence to objectivity. It concerns religion, and art, ritual and magic . . . science, on the other hand is born in opposition to it as the demythologization and 'disenchantment' of the world.[18]

The development of a theory of collective memory was therefore one other and similar way in which the mythic and enchanted world, alive within secular, rational modernity, was affirmed. Arguably Halbwachs was concerned to see what of the immutably human could remain in a modern world where change seemed to be the only constant. David Adams Leeming, in a study of the centrality of the voyage between worlds in ancient myth, suggests that these epics touched on the real significance of myth in connecting us to a pre-subjective condition:

> it is when we lose our ability to feel the mythic that we lose contact with that which is most basically and universally human. In a real sense a society loses its soul when it can no longer experience myth.[19]

You might turn the question that interested Halbwachs on yourself: what kind of recollection might be available to you outside of the unconscious, unacknowledged 'work' at the upkeep of memory that you engage with in relation to the collective dimensions of your life? The stories told and repeated within the family, and even within cultures, nations and so on, create pathways that make it possible to encounter – or, perhaps, impossible not to encounter – a past that is never entirely our own, and which is therefore 'mythological'. 'A child of nine or ten years old possesses many recollections', Halbwachs notes:

> What will this child be able to retain if he is abruptly separated from his family, transported to a country where his language is not spoken, where neither the appearance of people and places, nor their customs, resemble in any way that which was familiar to him up to this moment?[20]

The answer is: not much. What is lost is the means of transmitting knowledge, experience and memory. There is, in other words, no way to connect to the 'self-image' of the collective group, which provides the necessary sense of recognition – of being where one belongs – that would seem to be the immutable ground of that which is immemorial, and also of memory as an awareness of the distance between the present and the past. Halbwachs' view is expressed neatly in the words of Jan Assmann:

> Every individual memory constitutes itself in communication with others. These 'others', however, are not just any set of people, rather they are groups who conceive their unity and peculiarity through a common image of the past.[21]

So here we are again, back on the territory of the *image* of the past, which we can see is an *idea* (or even idealization) that works in the service of the present. It functions in the Durkheimian sense of a collective conscious and, as Assman would have it, enters the territory of myth precisely because it is 'remembered, narrated, and used', which is to say 'woven into the fabric' of a group's present.[22] This mythic relation to the past, therefore, is of a different order of engagement than we find with history. History presumes to engage with what is no longer present at the level of the factual, and as such embodies an aim that seems at some remove from the imperatives or needs of these collective representations, which are concerned after all with a spiritual kind of sustenance. In simple terms, this just means that what takes place with the latter is a kind of ritualistic (in the most everyday, as well as the strongest sense of that term) conjuring up of an image of the past whose accuracy is not at all relevant to the kind of power it effects in the present moment of its celebration. Emile Durkheim's notion of society itself therefore emerges as the engendering of a peculiar kind of myth that 'obligates people' to reawaken previous events in their lives and 'touch them up, shorten them, or complete them so that however convinced we are that our memories are exact, we give them a prestige that reality did not possess'.[23]

But the collective memory of Halbwachs is nonetheless routine life – the everyday – and is embodied and lived as a kind of time that exists on a different plane from that of history. It is simply the case that it might contain nothing remarkable enough to warrant the attention of an historian. This was a fact Halbwachs recognized, and was keen to stress, in differentiating collective memory from history:

> History is not interested in these intervals when nothing apparently happens, when life is content with repetition . . . without rupture or upheaval. But the group, living first and foremost for its own sake, aims to perpetuate the feelings and images forming the substance of its thought.[24]

Thus where history, as we saw, is marked by change – by leaps – collective memory, calling upon the structures of myth, could be characterized by its striving after stability and permanence; by a yearning for home. This is why the physical environment to which a group claims affinity becomes immensely important to a sense of collective memory. Its 'impassive' stones, walls and homes, for instance, appear to remain constant amid other potential upheavals:

> The nation may be prone to violent upheavals. The citizen goes out, reads the news, and mingles with groups discussing what has happened. The young must hurriedly defend the frontier. The government levies heavy taxes that must be paid. But all these troubles take place in a familiar setting that appears totally unaffected.[25]

It is when these settings are altered that we are able to glimpse how potent a collective sense of memory there may be in communities where the tide of history is resisted.[26] We can see an illustration of how this collective self-image works if we consider the recent travails of Northern Ireland's enigmatically named 'Historical Enquiries Team', which one British newspaper described as 'a *Waking the Dead*-style unit tasked with investigating unsolved crimes of the Troubles'.[27] The allusion to a popular British TV series about the investigation of so-called 'cold cases' was apt, given how this kind of memory work so often disturbs the present in the manner of raising ghosts. In the case of Northern Ireland it is the vestiges of divergent collective memories that are brought into collision. The example is also useful in that it represents a wider cultural trend towards 'historical' reassessment that is really tampering with powerful collective myths. 'Waking the dead', in this case, stirs up memory to effect a new and purifying forgetting, as one peculiar yet increasingly common instance of how managing memory becomes a phenomenon that marks Western societies that have been compelled – for one reason or another – to address the consequences of a colonial past. Such well-intentioned efforts hold out the promise of forgiveness and amnesty (a word, it is worth noting, etymologically related to *amnesia*, or forgetting).[28]

In contemporary Northern Ireland the work of investigators in gathering up evidence of a contested past with an acknowledged combustible legacy was taken to be an attack on a community and its self-image. It was the fact that these investigations challenged a collective representation that had been accepted as natural, thus bringing it into the court of history, with its facts and evidence, that constituted the threat to the more diffuse and intangible truth of the *conscience collective*. It is the ungraspable nature of this collective memory that makes all the more enigmatic the means by which it is transmitted from one person to another, and from one generation to the next. This transmission belongs to what Giorgio Agamben calls the 'the tradition of the immemorial'.[29] It tells us, Agamben suggests, that what is accepted as tradition is fundamentally unquestioned, and in a sense has to remain so. 'Every specific tradition, every determinate cultural patrimony, presupposed the transmission of that alone through which something like a tradition is possible'.[30] In other words, tradition, as an aspect of the life of the collective, exists in the forms of language and culture. Because of its naturalness it slips below the level of conscious scrutiny and into the most automatic and reflexive of dispositions that in the transmission from one generation to another remain, in a sense, concealed; or, again, accepted unquestioningly.[31]

The efforts of the Historical Enquiries Team in this case had resulted in a public outcry, protests and spontaneous outbursts of violence and criminal damage to property. It was a response that raised the thought that even the designation of the investigating office as the 'Historical Enquiries Team', within this particular political context, suggested something possibly more menacing than was intended, as if modern-day counterparts of the men from the Inquisition were coming around to ask you what you were doing on some night in 1971, or 1983, or at another equally distant time and place now half-forgotten. But in this case history's object was not mere events that could become raw material ready to be worked into a creation that we tend to get confused with memory; rather, its object *was* memory, the *conscience collective*. This was akin to the understanding of what memory was for Nietzsche, when he wrote that it could only be reinforced, and thus guaranteed affirmation, by pain, violence and the remembrance of the sacrifices that bound people together in its mythical truths:

> Perhaps there is nothing more terrible and strange in man's pre-history than his technique of *mnemonics*. 'A thing must be burnt in so that it stays in the memory: only something which continues to hurt stays in the memory' – that is a proposition from the oldest (and unfortunately the longest-lived) psychology on earth . . . When man decided he had to make a memory for himself, it never happened without blood, torments and sacrifices: the most horrifying sacrifices and forfeits (the sacrifice of the first born belongs here), the most disgusting mutilations (for example, castration), the cruellest rituals of all religious cults (and all religions are, at their most fundamental, systems of cruelty) – all this has its origin in that particular instinct which discovered that pain was the most powerful aid to mnemonics.[32]

The danger inherent in disturbing ghosts of a collective past suggests that the wellspring of what Durkheim called the *conscience collective* is rooted in one or more traumatic events that threaten the existence of a collective, thus making it self-conscious, aware of the need to preserve its own uniqueness. In general, it seems that most of these traumas revolve around the breaking of the umbilical link to the primordial home. This is, or would be, the source of the pain that has to be overcome, yet paradoxically as part of that overcoming it creates the memory of that wound or trauma. Once overcome, the trauma constitutes for later generations the only connection to the 'memory'. Cathy Caruth observes that 'the historical power of trauma is not just that the experience is repeated after its forgetting, but that it is only in and through its inherent forgetting that it is first experienced at all.'[33] We might draw a parallel between what takes place in cases of collective memory and its traumas, and the Freudian view of repression at a subjective level.

Forgetting through the suppression of traumatic events was, for Freud, an act of deep burial in which the forgotten is merely concealed and left temporarily dormant beneath layers of more recent and more amenable memories. The aim of confronting the trauma is not only 'to fill in gaps in memory' but more proactively to face up to consciousness and its illusions and 'to overcome resistances due to repression'.[34] This gives such traumatic pasts all the more power to unsettle because, as we saw in the example of the voyager between worlds found in ancient epics, in connecting to 'another place and another time' these memories illustrate the power of forces beyond our control to exert a hold over the present.[35] For Hegel, the pre-eminent thinker of history as progress, ancient myths and epics, insofar as they are seen to call upon memory, reveal the dangers of dabbling with the past and disturbing the supposedly dormant or exhausted forces that were likely just lying in some temporary slumber, as if waiting to be roused. Thus it is 'through the mimesis of the "voice of the dead" (Mnemosyne, memory) that cuts a "ditch" in the earth, a rift or crack in time, [that] the dead return to seek revenge on the living.'[36]

The example of this Historical Enquiries Team reveals forgetting to be emblematic of our own historicity. Because of this doubled existence that moves between 'worlds' or temporalities, we seem often condemned to remember at first, but strangely, so that we can forget and then move on with life. Rather than history, or who and what lays claim to the past, being the preserve of the 'winners', the confrontation between history and memory in Northern Ireland represents in this case a metaphorical descent into the underworld. There, as in Hades, there are no victors; only those tormented by the past.

In this the Historical Enquiries Team was not unique. It follows the model and example of post-apartheid South Africa's Truth and Reconciliation Commission, as well as the increasingly familiar instances of contemporary politicians apologizing for long-distant events they had no personal involvement in – British prime minister Tony Blair's apology in 2006 for Britain's involvement in the slave trade being once such example.[37] These are cases that illustrate the need history – understood as progress – has developed to accommodate traditions of collective memory. Like the Freudian practice that saw analyst and patient working through traumatic events and incorporating them into a narrative that released the grip of some personal 'hell' of a past – freedom from those apparently dead but still lingering memories – these political acts of remembering and forgetting remove the collective trauma and quarantine it within the official record, the archive. It becomes not just a library of facts or source of insights into events now past, but the means for containing the potentially toxic, combustible memories.

Urban Mnemonics, Social Amnesia

In Antonioni's *Blow-Up*, we see a dramatization of something we all too easily remain unaware of: the depth of reality that is concealed and enmeshed within habit, expectation and the surface order of life. The photographer, Thomas, was only able to penetrate this with the aid of a mechanical eye that records – memory-like – the reality we remain oblivious to. To live a *modern* life, as we have seen, is to experience varying degrees of self-loss and self-enhancement. It is the experience of inhabiting dense and impersonal networks which, in their growth and development, thicken the fabric of reality. By contrast, we may seem merely travellers on the surface of life – amnesiacs – oblivious to the depersonalized and implicit working memory writ large in the dense urban environments that carry us back and forth on our voyages and journeys. In the language of Deleuze and Guattari this would be described as an example of the so-called 'plane of immanence', a space or process of organization characterized by 'relations or movement and rest, speed and slowness between unformed elements' that amounts to 'subjectless individuations that constitute collective assemblages'.[38]

Looking at the situation from a more anthropological point of view, life in this environment, which we should think of as an ecology, a life-support system, not only becomes the source of a habitual existence, but exists *as* habitus – as a world that we come to feel at home in. But here space is subtly organized by a system of mnemonics that we can easily fail to take notice of. The sign that in its use of language, typeface, colour and symbolism warns you that you must take care or you may come to harm recognizes two things. First, it tells us that as we occupy and move around our cities and through our communication networks, we are frequently at the mercy of distractions; and second, that we thus require reminders that call us to attention. Marc Augé understandably terms such places of transit the 'non-places' of contemporary life:

> Space, as frequentation of places rather than a place, stems in effect from a double movement: the traveller's movement, of course, but also a parallel movement of the landscapes which he catches only in partial glimpses, a series of 'snapshots' piled hurriedly into his memory and, literally, recomposed in the account he gives of them . . . Travel constructs a fictional relationship between gaze and landscape.[39]

Such a space of *frequented places*, as long as it continues to permit passage, to work as a kind of support system for us, conceals the frailty of an existence that institutes a selective forgetting through our reliance on the efficacy of the entire ecology it goes into comprising.

It is no different, really, from the mnemonics of waste management; which is to say, just as the flush of a toilet removes for each of us the question of what to do with our waste (it 'vanishes' to be taken care of by a kind of invisible social rationality), so the existence of

'All attention demands some memory, and often when we are not admonished, so to speak, and warned to pay attention to certain of our present perceptions, we let them pass without reflexion and even without noticing them.' G. W. Leibniz, *New Essays on Human Understanding* (1704).

this urban plane of immanence, which comes to be through our life among traffic signals, road signs, geo-locational devices and so on, erases the anxiety or insecurity we may feel when in motion on those mini-voyages between the domestic and public spheres.

But the spatial formations that emerge here are underpinned by the rationalization of cities. On the surface of the city, memory is written not just in the names that commemorate people and events and mark places or locations, but in the unremarkable urban 'furniture' that offers a practical, 'how-to' kind of knowledge. This is the stuff of habit. Anything that allows us to displace effort creates a desire for more of the same. There is thus a dependency on this strange forest of abstract and often blunt symbols – the figures of depersonalized men, women and children assailed by lightning bolts and falling trees or pictured at the mercy of slippery floors. The evidence of how selectively stupefied modern life makes us not only puts to one side various doubts and uncertainties about traversing heavily populated and often hazardous public spaces where accidents seem to lie in wait; it might also lure us into a more complacent slumber we are only awoken from when something apparently random, aberrant or catastrophic happens. The increased anxiety about travel that took hold in the wake of the terrorist attacks of 9/11 (to name but one event) demonstrated that we are now more aware than at any time in the recent past that these non-places rely on the proper functioning of some invisible machinery that institutes a memory-system for immanent life, or life on the surface.

An example drawn from personal experience can illustrate how commonplace our selective amnesia is; how easily it is induced by the ways in which we relax into the repetitions of habit. Every morning at 08:05 a passenger train would leave the village of Carstairs for Glasgow, its destination some 30 miles away in central Scotland. Unusually, it was the only passenger train to begin its journey from this station, carrying the small number of commuters who lived there to workplaces in the city. The lack of frequency in this sparse schedule had always been a source of confusion, especially among train drivers for whom encounters with this particular route would be rare and consequently seemingly never fully solidified into the kind of habitual awareness that characterized the ease with which more familiar routes were undertaken and remembered. An equally notable consequence of these circumstances was the apparent conviction of passengers waiting at the first station stop down the line that this train – the 08:05 – would first collect and then deposit them safely in the city, conveniently within reach of their final destinations. At a time when British Rail promoted itself with adverts proclaiming that the train would 'take the strain', who can blame them? But the extent to which the passengers had sometimes misguidedly come to rely on events following the prescribed course was evident in their own absent-mindedness. There was no need to fret over details like the arrival of the train (though it may occasionally run a few minutes late), and so people might stand around on the platform reading newspapers, talk with fellow passengers or retreat into the enclosure of some small bubble of personal space entered through the invitation of a portable device (the iPod oblivion we have already encountered). I was witness, indeed, to the minor eruptions that unsettled the placid expectations of the passengers on those rare occasions when the 08:05 from Carstairs would (from my position inside the clerk's office where I worked at the time) mercilessly thunder through my station, the driver having no knowledge – or perhaps forgetting – that this was a stop on his route. Sitting blankly in his cab, perhaps, he could have no regard either for the torrent of complaints that would mere moments later be volleyed across the tracks at me as I stood on the platform to shout across that yes, dear passengers, *your* train just tore through this station and through your plans, and no, it would not be able to reverse and so the only thing to do was wait until the next one came along.

What such incidents speak of is the extent to which we – networked and interdependent – tacitly accept that normal social functioning rests on being able to forget about those things that we are unable to exercise control over. The reason this is the case is that there is so much that could possibly cloud out our attention, or leave us in a stupor. Our acceptance of such circumstances corresponds to the existence of those structures, networks and people who enable us to move around, yet who also easily blend into the background into the space beyond normal awareness. We are where we are because of them and they exist because of us and, in a sense, absorb certain of our wishes and desires. But, like the attention we pay to the locomotion of the human body, we often only become fully conscious of existence in this ecology when it breaks down.

When the daily trips into this realm of forgetting are interrupted, we are able to glimpse the alternate, suppressed network of causes in which we, as passengers on the surface, are really caught, and which exposes the illusion that we live in control of our destinies. At these points of breakdown, habit makes us passive subjects, but even in normal circumstances, as Bruno Latour would say, given our agency within an arrangement of forces that have an ability to act, which can be human or non-human, we may end up as merely one of many 'actants' (entities that act and are acted upon) that makes up a heterogeneous actor-network.[40]

The apparent continuity of the objective social world – or life on the surface, on the plane of immanence – can also be thought of as a projection of space and time in terms of the psychological orientation of the one who moves through it. It consists in the adjustment of consciousness within the causal expectations of the network as a force of life. Thus in important respects the *passivity* of a traveller in this kind of ecology develops through a conscious detachment from it: an awareness of self as an entity that is in some respects has to be kept separate from – almost floating on top of – a conjunction of forces whose impact on the psyche, as the sociologist Georg Simmel recognized, can be devastating. His elaboration of the conditions of the 'mental life' of the modern individual, Anthony Vidler notes, posited 'spatial isolation as a kind of prophylactic against psychological intrusion'.[41] We can glimpse this in the ways in which we come to occupy what we might term a 'third space'. This would refer to a space that cannot be identified in terms of either subjective or objective images of the individuated self, but which rather develops as a *response* to what Harvie Ferguson describes as 'the continuous flux of subjectivity' – a characteristic of modern experience which threatens the self-image of the body as existing as centred and immanently directed within the potential chaos.[42]

In Geoff Ryman's novel *253* we see a series of examples of the psychological projection of this 'third space', through the thoughts of the two hundred and fifty-three people of the book's title, who are passengers on board a London Underground train. Ryman's short, one-page sketches of the kind of social encounters marked by blasé responses, silences and diversionary actions amid the sensory bombardment of the busy train and its sights and sounds offer amusing glimpses of monadic existences brought close to collision. In Ryman's curious anatomy of each passenger, their identities are laid bare in a characterization of three short parts. The final impression we are left with seems to correspond to what is going on in the individual's third space (the other two offering objective and subjective images, respectively), thus perhaps offering confirmation of the slumber we fall into before consciousness rises to attention. As we reach passenger number eleven in the first car of the train, Mr Douglas Higbee, we learn the following:

Outward appearance
Blandly British, about thirty, plump, moustache, no chin. Black trousers, huge winter coat, blue shirt collar. A large overnight case. Appears to be asleep, except that one eye is open.

Inside information

Mr Higbee is the bar piano player on a cross-Channel ferry. His bag contains a change of underwear, a top hat, and home-produced cassettes which he offers for sale at the top of his piano. No one ever buys them. Like Superman, his costume, a tuxedo, is under the ordinary coat.

What he is doing or thinking

He is trying to avoid having to talk to the ship's magician, Passenger 18, who is also in the same carriage. Douglas has nothing against the magician. They have to spend a lot of time in the same bar and cabin being professionally pleasant to each other. You hardly want to be pleasant all the way from Waterloo to Dover as well. Douglas finds it difficult to be pleasant.[43]

My own observations of the habitual forgetting that seemed, depending on the circumstances, to be both a blessing and a curse of daily travel was replaced by a newer and more distant perspective. I disappeared into the dense 'thickness' to the anonymity of the signal centre, with its promise of controlling this one facet of the immanent disorder. Within my limited domain of control (amounting only to a few miles, I freely admit) I operated the switches and levers of my equipment in an effort to ensure the disturbances to the third space of the passenger were minimized.

✳

'UNLIKE BAUDELAIREAN MODERNITY', Augé suggests, non-places 'do not integrate the earlier [anthropological] places; instead these are listed, classified, promoted to the status of "places of memory", and assigned to a circumscribed and specific position.'[44] While this is true, the experience of life in non-places relies on memory-images of another kind, and these are complementary to the reality of life 'on the surface'. Objective images of non-place that at some level end up as an externalized memory of place are not the object or outcome of any singular experience but are nonetheless both represented and recognizable to us, even when presented in the most abstract forms, and suggest that the habitus or ecology of forgetting is transformed into something akin to home; which is to say, the ecology that in the end existence depends on and with which we reach an accommodation. The shape and form of these representations, however, can only be the product of a privileged and disembodied observer (that is, one who does not really exist) removed to a distance suitable enough to produce the scope of objectification to gather impressions of an entity the size of a city. What such an image would be is clearly removed from the finely grained 'reality' of our everyday lives, as given content by subjective experience. Yet, where they exist, it is such objective 'images' that become most memorable within the possible confusions of a reality that is always in motion. These are well known to any traveller and city-dweller – in the form, for example, of maps, tourist guides and now geo-locational devices (smartphone mapping applications, for instance). Yet it is from a rather different kind of objectification that we might see something of the forgetting and passivity that marks much contemporary existence.

In a series of remarkable illustrations of the 'surfacing' I have been trying to describe, Godfrey Reggio's unusual film *Koyaanisqatsi* (1983) uses photography and the movie camera positioned at elevated positions to provide an often omniscient sweep through modern human life. It seems, moreover, to present a kind of zoological vision of the networked and interdependent human in motion within its ecology; this is a film totally devoid of voices, testimonies or narration, which instead presents a succession of images of mute individuals and gatherings of people, sometimes just going about their business and often remaining portrait-still for the camera, with a look of almost vacant passivity. The sense of the plane of immanence that Deleuze and Guattari theorize, which whirls all around, is apparent throughout Reggio's highly idiosyncratic suggestion that the human habitus, if looked at a certain way, resembles the ecologies of the natural world. This is one reason the phenomena he presents seem to recall the kind of unconscious movement we see in flocks of starlings, or in a herd of buffalo on the move, or in bees at work and so on.

It seems impossible to watch the stunning sequence of Los Angeles traffic at night – all 'neon' tubes of colour forming long lines and then breaking abruptly – without thinking that what we see is the

Still from *Koyaanisqatsi* (dir. Godfrey Reggio, 1983).

work of a singular, unified intention. By dwelling on the spectacle of the freeways of the city, Reggio carries the viewer into what is a familiar world, but re-presents it, by speeding up motion, as an infinitely strange ecology of habit and repetition; a place that would seem to have no need for organic memory. As on the roads, so on the public transit systems: the interior of a station, viewed as a container for anonymous bodies entering and leaving from all sides, as if without aim, but always avoiding the obstacles formed by the movements of others; always with enough unconscious cooperation going on that the throng never descends into disorder.

Such an image of the human ecology might prompt us to see our own subjective and narrowed perspective as an exaggeration of equal measure. Somewhere in between the two there is Kevin Lynch's notion of the image of the city. It accords with the idea of a memory-image, easily recollected and offering the familiarity of something close to home. What we have is the mosaic of knowledge and memory that emerges from often anonymous exchanges, fortuitous encounters as one takes a train or a taxi, or asks a stranger for directions. 'The public image of any city' is therefore 'the overlap of many individual images.'[45] Once again, we might draw an analogy with ancient Greek ideas of anamnesis. The idea that all knowledge is actually a kind of recollection is realized in a peculiar way when the modern voyager moves through these urban ecologies, marked as they are by access to a kind of collective memory that is the source of our habitual dependence and amnesia.

The material form and evidence of this could be the justly famous diagrammatic map of London Underground, designed by an engineer named Harry Beck in 1933. It presents a visual arrangement of its particulars in a way that is far easier to remember than many alternative objectifications of place or terrain because it strips out all the unnecessary details that might get in the way of efficient 'surfacing'. In the rather simple form, colours and graphical arrangement of its features, what is displayed is a well-ordered image of Greater London in which all its parts have been equally spaced for our convenience (or so it seems), as if a sovereign designer had actually rearranged the city as a model of harmony. This map brilliantly demonstrates the hope of order over the fragmented and disjunctive reality of London, a city of unexpected dead ends, alluring avenues and promising trails that can easily pull one off-course.[46] As a representation of place, however, it is somewhat duplicitous in its vision of good order, as Adrian Forty notes:

> For all its clarity, [the map] is highly misleading; unlike the previous maps, which represented stations in their correct geographical positions, the new map not only reorganised the lines along horizontal, vertical or 45 degree axes, but also enlarged the distance between the stations in the central area, and reduced that between stations in the outer area . . . by making the distance between the suburbs and the centre look so small [it] induced people to undertake journeys they might have otherwise hesitated to make.[47]

The map, in fact, resembles an electrical circuit diagram, and looks very much like the displays that are found in the signal centres from which rail traffic is controlled. Yet however misleading it is, the image of this ordered space has become part of a common perception of London, and has served as the model for similar transit maps the world over. Its success is found in the fact that the urban topography is refashioned as an *objectified* form that supports our movements, one that comes complete with temporary relations of identity (in the form of stations and interchanges) that substantiate our everyday causal expectations (meeting a friend, getting to work on time and so on) and carry forward the life of both individual and city.

It provides an interesting contrast with travels into less 'imageable' environments. In the popular imagination, for instance, the open road symbolizes something quite distinct from the kind of repetition we have been considering; it promises instead a more existential kind of forgetting in the quick erasure of one's past – think of all of those Bruce Springsteen songs about the road as a means to slip free of an unwanted fate ('Born to Run'), or Kerouac's *On the Road* as the Romantic imagination given written form – and with the aim of drawing a line under the deadly continuity of everyday habits and rhythms.

A certain idealized vision of the road, unsurprisingly, invests it with a 'libertarian ideal' of unfettered free movement.[48] Thus 'driving' – as opposed to travelling as a passenger – also describes voyages of discovery or possibly disorientation (consider the use of the word 'trip' to describe the experiences induced by the drug LSD) because the extension of a space beyond what is taken to constitute the plane of immanence suggests a mode of transcendence. It is not often, after all, that we visualize an open road as something that heads *backwards*, as opposed to thinking of 'the road' as the forward extension of a space that speaks of possibility. The 'road less travelled' contains novelty and is therefore usually more remarkable. Our urban mnemo-technics, by contrast, consists of an abundance of signs and prompts simply because the passivity these very spaces engender makes us forgetful of *ourselves*. This is clearly one of the reasons travellers at airports and transit terminals the world over are also subjected to continual reminders to obey commands that are already present everywhere as visual reminders ('Don't park in the drop zone'; 'Don't leave your luggage unattended'; 'Stay clear of the end of the platform' and so on). That this all works is testament to a rather different kind of collective memory than that proposed by Halbwachs or Benjamin; this, rather, is memory as collective intelligence dispersed into the ecology of contemporary life, and thus hidden in plain sight.

Digital Delirium

The contemporary urban experience of time and space as conditions that produce amnesia might refocus attention on the modern notion of the self-moving individual inherited from Descartes, which is complicated by the ways we live today. In a sense, life is overcome by the daily practicalities of living within societies that have grown complex, and exhibit an interconnectedness that a philosopher of the seventeenth century could not have anticipated. To understand memory as something in the possession of the individual, as a product of mind, does not mesh with our reality now. Where now, we might wonder, do we find the mind that can doubt the existence of everything apart from its own thoughts? The answer, it seems, is nowhere – especially when it seems that the possible contents of the mind (that is, the available experiences) have found a home in extensions of our physical being; add-ons, plug-ins and other technical prostheses. The body that houses the mind, as we have seen, moves in a time and space that is heterogeneous, interdependent and which, in a sense, catches us within its web of connections. Our knowledge of this world already depends on and accesses something akin to an external 'memory', one that is inseparable from how experience – the past experience of others, the potential experience of abstract, hypothetical, individuals or users – becomes remade as information that can be easily accessed and consulted as the product of an anonymous collective intelligence. Something roughly similar to this has been revolutionizing the life of memory in a more thoroughgoing way. Since roughly the second half of the twentieth century, in particular, the modern idea of the individual has been undergoing its own revolutionary re-evaluation. This is because as we extend memory into technical objects and network relations clearly existing outside of the body, we ourselves become points or nodes in technical networks. This ensures that 'the process of acquiring, storing and transmitting information', which has now become a necessary requirement of normal social functioning, is a process that

> flows through us . . . and involves not only all of the present
> and past society but also the whole of what we call the world

> . . . what each of us calls 'I' is a knot of relations that, when unravelled, reveals itself to have no hook on which these relations may hang.[49]

In other words, the individual has no unique, individuated existence within these relations and connections. The chief analyst of how 'networked' (in the broadest sense) modern life has become is the French sociologist-philosopher Bruno Latour, who in his work on actor-networks arguably offers a more compelling picture of what it means to be human within these contexts than do long-standing modern notions of *self, individual* or *subject*. What we have to understand is not in fact a mere human condition, but the conditions through which life has become directly lived through a host of human/non-human interfaces. In that sense, Latour argues, 'to define humans is to define the envelopes, the life support systems, the *Umwelt* that makes it possible for them to breathe.'[50]

But we should not lose sight of the fact that we extend into the world, so to speak, and gain access to an ecology of memory by connecting with 'organic', human networks as well as technological, 'non-human' ones. The first category encompasses communities (in the sense Durkheim understood them, as the embodiment of a living collective memory), and this extends beyond to social structures, media and the real and virtual spaces we live in more generally. Acts of remembering depend on establishing a connection to the world beyond – to produce a social relation, in other words – as Nikolas Rose has argued:

> For something to be remembered it must first be given the status of an experience, then made available for reactivation through pledges, rituals, songs, pictures, libraries, contracts, debts, the design of buildings, the structuring of space and time and much more.[51]

Yet for all the evidence that whatever memory is, it is as much *out there* in the world as it is inside our heads (the two cannot be separated), we are nonetheless apt to fall back on the idea of some core mental activity that we associate with learning, remembering and recollecting – some notion of 'organic' memory – which, in short, is a mechanism for storage and recollection. It is no surprise, then, that we often imagine that it resembles 'retrieval mechanisms, stores, data banks, and so on'.[52] It just so happens that the stuff of this kind of memory is not the large mainframe computers or retrieval databases of the mid-to-late twentieth century, but the technologies that now define the space of *personal* computing. So, to give an account of what there is out there in the lifeworld that has come to occupy a space we call 'memory', we have to consider the non-human extensions that we have come to depend on, and which – through advances in communications and network technologies – are quickly becoming very human in the simple sense that we feel at home with them, and they are ever more tailored to our needs.

When we come to the seemingly infinite digital vault of today – which first shrinks dramatically in physical dimensions and then seems to vanish into a virtual cloud – the 'conflation of memory and storage' becomes glaringly obvious as the relation that 'both underlies and underlines digital media's archival promise'.[53] What this means is very simple: the very existence of digital media, its raison d'être, what it is and what it does, is as intimately bound to notions of memory that have been carried over from our pre-digital under-standing of memory as the notion of memory as the unifying characteristic of the self was in centuries past. The difference is that digital media offer a glimpse of a space that seems to keep expanding, and to which obstacles and barriers to access seem to be vanishing:

> The major characteristic of digital media is memory. Its ontology is defined by memory, from content to purpose, from hardware to software, from CD-ROMs to memory sticks, from RAM to ROM. Memory underlies the emergence of the computer as we know it . . .[54]

We might wonder how it came to this. Consider for example, the startling evidence of how limited this archival promise was in the early years of the desktop computer, which, after all, is the point at which everyday experience and memory begins to be remade with the aid of external storage mechanisms.

At the dawn of this age, in the 1980s, the cost of memory – or disk storage capacity – reflected how scarce a commodity this new-fangled outsourced memory could be. An advert clipped from an old magazine 30 years ago reveals that one megabyte could effectively cost around $500. According to an estimate published in the technology magazine *Wired*, that same amount of money in 2007 could buy a device with capabilities that likely would have been unimaginable a few decades ago:

> a 750 gigabyte drive or a 3 gigahertz processor . . . over 15 years that's an advance of 7,500 times for the hard drive [memory storage capacity] and 60 times for the processor [speed of retrieval, among other functions].[55]

Expressed in other terms, the megabyte that in the early 1980s was worth around $500 now costs approximately one hundred-thousandth of a cent. This apparent dwindling of costs reflects not how valueless digital memory is, but rather how much more of it a few decades worth of developments in computer engineering has been able to produce. The existence of all this capacity, of course, marks a real revolution in how we 'remember' and, even more so, what kind of things are saved to this memory. In the end, it seems, its logic is to 'remember' everything.

✳

THE DIGITAL ERA's equivalent of Lord Elgin – whose appropriation of fragments from the Acropolis has been thought of as both an act of cultural preservation and theft – no longer needs to remove valuable artefacts from their habitat, nor even to restrict themselves to quaint forms of representation such as photography or film. No, because of the abundance of this inexpensive memory, they can scan and record every millimetre of under-threat cultural heritage sites. One example of how such an objective might be carried through to realization is offered by CyArk, a digital preservation project based in California which has undertaken to digitally scan and 'save to memory' hundreds of such sites. This kind of preservation – monumental in scale – was driven by a desire to avoid a repeat of the infamous destruction of the Buddhas of Bamiyan in Afghanistan in 2001, as CyArk's founder told *Wired* magazine:

> What the Taliban did to the Bamiyan Buddhas in 2001 made me realise that nothing can replace those monuments, that past. If we'd had some high-resolution 3-D scans, they wouldn't have been so completely obliterated from the earth.[56]

Through developments such as CyArk, unimaginable a generation ago, the outsourcing of memory can now take numerous forms, from the rudimentary – knots in rope, marks on a surface, writing – to the detailed complexity of the digitization of reality in applications such as Google Earth. Externalizing memory always served a need that the mere unaided organic memory was likely incapable of meeting on its own. All that has changed today is the level of need, which is driven by an overwhelming sense of impending loss that marks memory as a subject of literary and philosophical interest as far back as we care to look, but which is driven today by the feeling that everything must be 'backed up', just because it can be. Those external hard drives and memory sticks you see lying around your desk, along with your cloud-stored data (video, photographs, documents, calendars), now accessible through handy mobile devices and portable computers that go everywhere with you, enlarge and amplify the qualities and functions that have always been sought in trying to cope with the frailty of an unaided memory.

Before writing was widely available it was a need met, Jean-Pierre Vernant tells us, in a different way and with an external memory determined by available means. The ancient Greeks found their own version of external memory in the form of an individual who was called a *mnemon*, one who remembers: a kind of memory-man (they were usually male). Like our contemporary external memory devices, the *mnemon* was there as a kind of backup for the important details, and because he could be accessed easily, he was even – like our own externalized memory – taken on travels. More specifically, it was within the legal system that *mnemon*s undertook to remember the past for the sake of settling legal disputes; later they had a seemingly more elevated role as 'magistrates responsible for the preservation of written records'.[57] In all cases their functions revolved around remembering. In yet other accounts, particularly drawing from mythology, the *mnemon* was 'the servant of the hero whom he constantly accompanies in order to remind him of the divine mission that will cause his death if he forgets it'.[58]

Today, no attempt to stay on top of every experience that might be an object worthy of remembering can do without a means of storage and transmission that extends far beyond the human, and without digital and virtual memory. A few decades ago, the future was still thought of in cyborgian or robotic images. 'Another change to be expected', Vilém Flusser wrote in 1990, 'is the coupling of electronic memories with robots.'[59] But rather than the kind of sci-fi existence this may conjure up in the imagination, the reality has quickly become familiar, even mundane. 'Electronic' memory ends up coupled to robots only in the sense that computers, networks and cloud servers become interfaces to non-human life that allow us to feel as if we are in touch with our data, and the world's (that is, our new electronic memory), wherever we go. Thus the current state-of-the-art memory-aid application (or app) Evernote promotes its potential to the everyday user, whose life consists of much movement and 'surfacing', beneath the kind of slogan that promises a solution to living within a world defined by the excess of phenomena, of potential experiences and infinite information: 'Remember Everything'. Just like an elephant – Evernote's icon and product identity – the use of this application will see to it that you will possess a memory that neutralizes the danger of forgetting. Its purpose is to allow you to 'connect to your external brain' and of course, to 'access your memories'.[60]

This, though, is merely one example of the kind of software that is being designed for life on the move, and lived through multiple user interfaces that all have to connect to the same external memory. These are actually lifestyle add-ons that capture, store and retrieve information and experiences in almost any medium: in text that is entered manually, in handwriting that is photographed and scanned with text-recognition software, in photographs, video, sound and anything that can be snatched or clipped from the Internet, with the ease of taking a snapshot with a dumb camera.

To never forget anything has been an aim of computer engineers at least since the possibilities of networked digital life became apparent in the last decade or so. So-called 'life-logging', or the real-time recording of one's entire life, as practised by the Microsoft engineer Gordon Bell, attempts to integrate within everyday life a variety of technologies for remembering whose use will become routine and habitual, and takes the desire to remember to new – and, some might say, pathological – levels of particularity.[61] Life-logging adds something new to the burgeoning infinite library (or cultural archive) promised by increased data storage, and by search engines for finding and recalling information. It is driven by the belief that what continues to elude the grasp of external memory as a mere storage mechanism that may preserve anything that can be digitized, is the intangible, ephemeral *everydayness* of everyday life. What shoes you were wearing on a particular day; what you were thinking or doing at a specific time on that day; what you watched on TV; who you spoke to as you went about your business; and so on. While Gordon Bell was motivated partly by his work as an engineer with Microsoft, his 'MyLifeBits' project was driven also by a sense of the effect ageing was beginning to have on his life. In the realization that with 'each day that passes, I forget more and remember less', he saw a need to remember more and more.

Just as Google Earth gathers more and more data to produce a more detailed snapshot of the world than has ever been seen, so, with the aid of a range of memory prostheses, it became possible for Bell to develop 'a digital diary or e-memory' that would be used 'continuously as you go about your life'.[62] It aimed to mesh seamlessly with normal routines, supported by an array of equipment of the kind once only dreamed of by spies and security services:

> an assortment of tiny, unobtrusive cameras, microphones, location trackers, and other sensing devices that can be worn in shirt buttons, pendants, tie clips, lapel pins, brooches, watchbands, bracelet beads, hat brims, eyeglass frames, and earrings. Even more radical sensors will be available to implant inside your body, quantifying your health. Together with various other sensors embedded in the gadgets and tools you

use and peppered throughout your environment, your personal sensor network will allow you to record as much or as little as you want of what happens to you and around you.[63]

If that seems like a staggeringly ambitious effort to duplicate life, with all the 'insignificant' bits preserved, it is at least evidence of a trend towards tracking or logging even the most inconsequential events as a form of remembering, and in fulfilment of the logic of digital memory to offer the means, in a sense, to duplicate reality. At a less intensive level of engagement, but still acting as a kind of digital memory database that makes possible the recollection of one's life and doings, something similar is taking place with developments in social networking media. Facebook, with the introduction of 'timelines' – which can produce detailed chronologies reaching back to birth (all one has to do is fill in the gaps by adding photographic memories and other materials and information) – enables a user to 'return' to specific points in time. With add-ons like Intel's 'The Museum of Me', the entire archive of an individual's online social network – photographs and videos – can be remade as a tour of a virtual museum of a life and what was thought to be worth preserving.

Writing not long after the promise of digital life started to become apparent, R. U. Sirius, a commentator once described as the 'Clown Prince of the Digital Counterculture', predicted our disappearance into a kind of digital soup:

> The future, my cultured friends, is the direct interaction between the nervous system and the information system. The formerly interior terrain of thought and memory will be exteriorized. It will begin at our fingertips. Our experiences – far from being disembodied – will be one of direct bodily reception.[64]

If we consider the ways in which digital life has taken hold as the direct connection to a realm of aesthetic experience – the importance of sounds, touch and visual iconography to sense of being at one with technical objects and machines – it could be argued that the pursuit of the aesthetic was always implicit in the development of the Apple computer. Apple pioneered the idea of the personal computer as the link to an entire ecology of remembering and forgetting, specifically through its development of devices that successively became more intuitive, and ultimately touch-responsive, and so feeling at home with them was within the reach of even the most technologically inept (small children, elderly people). The entire Apple philosophy was driven by a desire to design an environment that would make the user feel at ease among what were previously machines that had seemingly no relation to human desires or wishes. The worst thing computers could do, in the view of Apple's chief ideologue, Steve Jobs, was to alienate their user. Hence the presentation of their first truly *personal* computer, the Macintosh, as something entirely detached from images of monolithic cabinets that concealed a mass of circuits and wires that only a technician could operate. Apple would offer devices that could become part of your life; devices which were aiming always to be responsive to a user's needs and even their sensitivities. 'Hello' was the simple slogan on the Macintosh computer of 1984, which established the template for everything Apple tried to do thereafter to make computers part of who we were and how we functioned in everyday life. The theme was underlined in the company's famous '1984' television advert, in which the world of non-Apple computing is represented by the Orwellian Big Brother who, through computing technology, had dominated and controlled us, and who had to be destroyed to liberate the masses.

Surf Life

While we may speak of digital memory as merely the latest form of externalized memory, the contemporary ecology of remembering and forgetting – extending to networks, technologies and applications that promise some kind of direct bodily reception – can no longer be thought of in terms of something that exists apart from us. We can no longer objectify it, simply because it is everywhere and increasingly pervasive in almost every aspect of day-to-day life. It is not some separate realm, as cyberspace may once have been conceived of, nor a mere access point that requires a definite act of logging in. Those descriptions might have applied to an understanding of the

Internet in the period of its early development. It is, rather, the very atmosphere we 'live and breathe', so to speak. It exists and expands as a form of digital memory, and we therefore come to exist as part of it. There is very little thinking in the modern Western tradition that has been able, or has even thought it necessary, to describe or think through a reality that exists beyond the subject/object distinction. That has begun to change in recent decades. As Michel Serres – a philosopher whose work could be said to embrace an ecological understanding of human life – has suggested, it might always have been the case that life is born amid a flux and 'noise' that comes to elude us. In our fondness for separating human experience from the non-human natural world, we come to ignore the ecological dimensions of that experience. But, Serres suggests, this separation is a kind of illusion arising from the necessity of disengaging from the too-muchness of reality:

> Water, the sea. Perceptional bursts, inner and outer, how can they be told apart? How am I to tell, any environment I've entered, become immersed in, that this wood I'm confronted with doesn't go on forever, that I'll get to the edge of the forest someday? I can't see the trees of this forest. A murmur, seizing me, I can't master its source, its increase is out of my control. The noise, the background noise, the incessant hubbub, our signals, our messages, our speech and our words are but a fleeting high surf, over its perpetual swell.[65]

'Surf Life' is what we might call the experiential dimension of the new immersive ecology of memory, simply because it gives in to what Serres calls 'perceptional bursts', and to 'noise', in order to live. It provides an 'atmosphere', a weather system of the everydayness of life.

In this sense, *surf* refers at once to the surfeit of memory and to a mode of existence that plays out, as we have seen, as a kind of 'surfacing' – a disengagement from the depth of life that we have come to associate with experiences that memory becomes fixed upon. Without differentiation, amid such 'noise', however, there is nothing for remembering to distinguish in perception – everything just is as it is, a condition of immanence. Even to speak of 'surfing' as a kind of activity – although one that slips into non-action – gets us close to the ecological dimensions of being at one with an environment we inhabit, however temporary the encounter might be.

Many years before we had fibre optic networks, or even an Internet to surf, Gilles Deleuze thought that there was something new, something to do with the nature of the kind of temporality we inhabit, that produced a need for a new kind of thought that could grasp the nature of an existence that unfolded in evanescent moments. 'The key thing', he said, 'is how to get taken up in the motion of a big wave, a column of rising air, to "get into something" rather than being the origin of an effort.'[66] He was referring to activities like surfing, hang-gliding and environment-immersive activities, which in the late twentieth century were becoming more widespread. The thinker – or philosopher – of this apparently new kind of existence, as Tom Conley notes in an introduction to Deleuze's *The Fold*, would also need to be a 'surfer'; which is to say, one who was able to leave aside distinctions between the mind and the world, or between subject and object – a geophilosopher who 'moves along the crest of turbulence, on the shoulders of waves that envelop mind, energy, and matter, and that diffuse them into the atmosphere.'[67]

We glimpse Surf Life in the everyday of Western urban existence, whose 'surfacing', as I have referred to it, is actually a kind of disengaged (but always implicitly connected) attitude or condition that spills over into forgetting as a response to the 'too-muchness' of contemporary life. The more significant counterpart to Surf Life now, of course, is the realm of digital memory and the way it has morphed into a more dense and heterogeneous kind of interrelatedness. As such, Surf Life will clearly live and thrive in ubiquitous computing, in smart mobile technologies and in the ambient space of the always-on network-as-atmosphere.

Media technologies that existed once to document and archive the world around us, providing external and physical counterparts to memory, are now designed for different purposes that implicitly recognize the existence of what I refer to as Surf Life. Their intention is to grasp the momentary and immersive, and for reasons that seem to have little to do with posterity – with the archival impulse – than it is with living in the now. A description of the ION Twin

Video, used by participants in immersive 'sports' such as surfing, is instructive:

> Twin Video is the world's first video recorder that allows you to capture both your world and your reaction to it. This revolutionary camera makes interviews, vlogs, and creating videos for YouTube and Facebook easy thanks to live-editing features that include picture swap, split screen, and picture in picture.[68]

Thus if you actually do film yourself surfing ocean waves, your surfing experience, once uploaded to the digital vault, also becomes part of the continual flow of possible experiences that might be encountered unthinkingly by a network surfer. But, more generally, what such devices tell us is that few of the old and long-standing metaphors through which memory was conceived – the archive, the image, the mystic writing pad and so on – are entirely adequate to understanding a reality in which experience can no longer be understood according to the kind of accounts that made it the basis of human memory; which is to say, memory understood as an effect of the accumulation of experience and, as such, the source of some kind of existential unity.

In philosophical reflection from Aristotle to Locke and, in many ways, right up to contemporary life, this conception of memory has largely held sway as a common-sense account. It depended nonetheless on an idea of what the grounds of experience were that no longer pertains today: a firm separation of the perceiving and experiencing self from the world that was the object *of* that experience. It is becoming more difficult to think of a self that exists apart from a supposed *object* that we would call 'the world', and it is one more reason that thinking of memory in terms of its various ecologies, or habitats, allows us to attempt to catch what is distinctive about a world in which memory inheres in all kinds of objects, surfaces and, indeed, permeates the air. To think in this way, Peter Sloterdijk remarks, is to reflect on the Greek notion of home or house, *oikos*, which perhaps helps us to understand how easy it becomes to feel at home in Surf Life:

> The beauty of the concept of the house is the fact that it can articulate the idea of reciprocal belonging between a place and its inhabitant. This 'house' prefigures the modern biologists' concept of the environment . . . according to which organisms and their environment are in a relation of mutual belonging. So modern ecology would be a science of general domestication.[69]

If we follow through on the need to think of home in this sense, then home is in both what we might associate with the immemorial and archaic *and* in whatever conditions emerge that offer the promise of overcoming the split in consciousness that produces memory first as the awareness of loss, and thus of finitude.

When the physical space of the exterior world is, in effect, connected to what we call memory, through ambient, invisible interfaces, whatever boundary was believed to have separated subject and object has disappeared. In a sense, you may now be at home wherever you are. Along with this realization, it seems, goes any meaningful distinction between remembering and forgetting. Why? The answer is simply because now when we forget, the chances are that something else we are 'plugged in' to is picking up the slack, potentially saving what otherwise might be lost, or obviating the need to even think in terms of loss, lack or separation. This is Surf Life.

All this is to say that to think about memory, if this is not now obvious, we have to move away from a kind of thinking that was once grounded in ideas of subjectivity and selfhood. This gets us a long way, historically speaking, but it does not, and cannot, encompass what memory has become, aided as it is by a universal, self-sustaining memory-intelligence embodied in the most everyday of objects, particularly smart mobile devices. Certainly, thinking of memory in terms of *self-identity* is a necessary prelude and complement to any later attempts to rethink the nature of memory in light of changing experience and new forms of cultural life, but the key issue is that thinking in terms of 'self' reflects a split from the world or a past that is now overcome – or, if not, it becomes increasingly irrelevant to the practice of everyday life. We only know what has changed in our experience of the world around us, in other words, by seeing the inadequacy of old thinking to an understanding of present circumstances. That does not mean that we turn our backs on thinking whose origins pre-date contemporary experience. On the contrary, a philosophical account of the nature of reality that might best enable us to form an understanding of our situation today pre-dates modernity, and was developed partly in response to John Locke's idea of memory as, variously, a blank slate, empty container or, indeed, a camera obscura on to which experience would be inscribed. I refer here to Gottfried Wilhelm Leibniz's notoriously obtuse theory of monads – his 'monadology' – which, by contrast with the Aristotelian cast of Locke's thinking on memory, could be said to have drawn rather more on Platonic notions of memory as anamnesis. The comparison suggests that a parallel tradition of speculative thinking about the nature of reality seems now to be confirmed, particularly in terms of how that reality is increasingly constituted as 'memory', and the ways in which we seem to reflect on or become absorbed by it. Leibniz, in other words, provides a means of thinking that accords with this Surf Life.

In responding to Locke at the turn of the eighteenth century, Leibniz would argue that where memory and perception were concerned, 'the question at issue' was 'whether the soul itself is entirely void, like a tablet whereupon nothing has yet been written'.[70] Here the term 'soul' seems clearly to be used in the ancient sense of the seat of memory, or the faculty of remembering and recollecting. Against Locke's view, he suggested that 'the soul contains originally the principle of various notions and doctrines, which external objects simply recall from time to time', and which could be thought of in terms of the recognition of the familiar:

> living fires, flashes of light, hidden within us, but caused to appear by the contact of the senses, like the sparks which the shock of the flint strikes from the steel. And it is not an unreasonable belief that these flashes are a sign of something divine and eternal.[71]

What is remarkable in the description of how we might conceive of such remembrance is not just the hint of Platonic anamnesis, but the fact that Leibniz's language is echoed much later in Walter Benjamin's theory of knowledge and remembrance. Benjamin, for instance, referred to dialectical images that contain a 'knowledge that only comes in lightning flashes' – as if to emphasize that after hundreds of years in which truth and knowledge have been thought of in terms of self, Leibniz suddenly appears as the crucial, but hidden, link to another history of modern memory; one that gets beyond subject and object, and in doing so sees not a world of individuals who exist over against the world, but persons who are relations and connections within it, and within histories laden with memory.[72]

It might have been the case that in its day Leibniz's theory of monadology jarred with the observable reality of a time that was moving away from theological views of reality; or that it seemed to grasp for something that might not be observable, verifiable, *there*, and was therefore out of step with the dominant empiricism of early modern thinkers, such as Locke. The work known as the 'Monadology' was in fact regarded in its day as 'puzzling and even paradoxical'.[73] Yet if it pointed to a mode of thinking that seemed to lack the clear-cut simplicity of Locke's philosophy, it nonetheless had more influence on later Romantic ideas about nature and the place of the human than the scientific developments that sprang from empiricism. This viewed the world not as *oikos*, as house or home, but as a resource to be exploited. In this respect, it may be the case that it has taken Leibniz's ideas – once shorn of their residual theology – some 400 years to be truly penetrating in their description of reality.

What has changed significantly, as we have seen, is that life now has to be understood in terms of a connectedness that we associate with networks and ambient spaces, and not least the rapidly expanding space of digital memory that underlies it all. If we look back to Leibniz's account of existence, the unity of being was understood as a reality that mirrored the mind of the infinite or, in other words, God. Today we seem to have devised the means towards our own infinite expansion into our atmosphere through our capacity to store infinite quantities of information, or 'memories'. Within the context of a pre-media age – a premodern age – where the all-knowing, all-remembering and infinite meant only one thing, the faithful had to trust in God, who, Peter Sloterdijk wryly notes, had 'no storage problems' and so could remember 'better than mundane media'.[74]

The idea of memory, as it relates to self-identity and to the implicit gap that we might perceive between our subjective presents and the past, relies fundamentally on separation (not connection) and on the self-awareness of experiencing at some level a kind of irrecoverable loss. On the basis of that understanding, we have memory because we have lost or become distanced from our origins, from the past and from the primordial home. This past is what tugs at us, and what impels memory to be understood as the core of self-identity in the modern world (a world, as we saw, defined by upheaval and separation, and the breaking of immemorial tradition).

The classical image of this separation, which we began with, is found in the tale of Odysseus and his battle against fate on his return home. The voyage home is itself the setting for most of the dramas in which a choice is made – very significantly – between mortality and immortality. In choosing mortality over the life of a god, the return home becomes the basis for understanding meaningful existence as a trial to overcome a variety of obstacles, or as a form of self-definition that emerges in the face of adversity. As Hans Blumenberg notes, it is an idea that goes deep to the core of Western thinking about what it means to be human. While humans 'live their lives and build their institutions on dry land', it seems often to be accompanied by a 'metaphorics of the perilous sea voyage', which runs right through Western thought:

> The repertory of this nautical metaphorics of existence is very rich. It includes coasts and islands, harbors and the high seas, reefs and storms, shallows and calms, sail and rudder, helmsmen and anchorages, compass and astronomical navigation, lighthouses and pilots. Often the representation of danger on the high seas serves only to underline the comfort and peace, the safety and serenity of the harbor in which a sea voyage reaches its end.[75]

Yet, as significant as the metaphorics of the sea voyage have become in thinking through the human condition, we should keep in mind that the ostensible point of the feats of endurance, bravery, determination and so on that give life to it all is the need to overcome some fundamental separation. It may be explicitly significant in its dimensions (as in the case of exile, imprisonment) or ill-formed and woozily nostalgic (yearning to be somewhere that we equate with happiness, a return to adolescence), but at the end always seems to be fixed on a time and a place that relates to some sense of feeling at home.

But we live now, without apparent anxiety, lives that make place or homeland – in the anthropological sense – relatively meaningless. The metaphorics of the sea voyage give way to alternatives that stress the condition of being at home as being in the midst of phenomena; being connected, yet also comfortably or unproblematically isolated within that interconnectedness. When Leibniz sought to outline the nature of a reality that was composed of minute phenomena – what he termed *petites perceptions* – that at once act upon us, and which we in some way reflect back, he seemed once again to be thinking in a way that allows us to begin to grasp the broader ecological character of contemporary life. One of the images he thought captured a sense of how infused with unconscious perception reality seemed to be was found in the sensory experience of waves crashing against the shore:

> To hear this noise as we do, we must surely hear the parts of which the whole is made up, that is to say the noises of each wave, although each of these little noises only makes itself heard in the confused combination of all the others together, that is to say in the actual roar and would not be noticed if the wave which makes it were the only one.[76]

We exist, in other words, with phenomena that work upon us at the level of sensation and emotion, and which hark back to pre-scientific notions of environment as the living habitat that is understood intuitively or without any recourse to conscious reflection. It arises from a belonging that erases any distinction between an individual (a modern notion) and place. Daniel Tiffany has linked Leibniz's monadology to a sense of our place in the world that has affinities with the desire to, in a sense, be rid of memory as the awareness of finitude. In other words, as a way of thinking of consciousness, of home, without falling back into the idea that we are alienated from some primordial home,

> Leibniz's theory of monadic perception . . . provided the philosophical rationale for placing sensation, intellection, and feeling on a continuum, so that perception and feeling might be regarded as 'confused' forms of thinking – and thinking as a species of 'perception'. In this respect, the 'Monadology' provides the basis for eighteenth-century conceptions of sentimentality, a discourse of 'intellectual feelings' and, hence, of objects, places, or events infused with emotional reflection.[77]

In a curious and roundabout way that runs via Walter Benjamin's own variant on monadic thinking. It is the implicit anamnesis – seen

Katsushika Hokusai, *The Great Wave off Kanagawa, c.* 1831–3, woodblock print. Human experience is transformed in contemporary life from what Hans Blumenberg called 'a metaphorics of the perilous sea voyage' (represented by the figures in the boats in Hokusai's famous print) into a metaphorics of surf, of atmospheres that reflect a merging of wave and environment that evokes the monadic nature of contemporary life and the interrelatedness implied by an infinite memory that strives for total presence. This is home, habitat and the new ecology of remembering and forgetting.

in remembrance as a kind of self-recognition that has momentarily been lost sight of – that underpins Benjamin's concept of messianic redemption.[78] Leibniz gives us access to a different kind of collective memory: one defined as monadic habitat. Today, the monadic life – Surf Life – is evident all around us. The Leibnizian unconscious, informed by *petites perceptions*, is naturally at home in momentary and passionate states which, Philip Fisher suggests, are 'configurations' of an 'underlying notion of a temporary state of a person'.[79] The metaphor of surf therefore refers not merely to the wave: it is the image of the wave that breaks into minute particles that presents us with a more accurate metaphor for these states of being.

If we now form, in contemporary Western societies in particular, part of this seemingly infinite network that constitutes an entire ecosystem, a new kind of habitat, then it has to change the nature of memory and, no less, what we refer to when we talk and think about memory. Leibniz clearly never used the language of networks and digital media, but he nonetheless was convinced of the connectedness of every soul, which is to say every monad. They existed within and as part of an infinity of minute perceptions that explained a 'pre-established harmony of soul and body, and indeed of all monads' that allow us to unthinkingly move through the time and space of the everyday. As Leibniz said, 'it is these minute perceptions which determine us in many experiences without our giving them a thought.'[80] In other words, perception understood in these terms does not work on memory in the same way as a camera obscura, which produces distinct forms or pictures. In Leibniz's conception, the monad is self-contained, 'windowless' (admitting no light, so to speak), yet it reflects the whole whose interrelatedness it partakes of; in fact, it would not exist without it.

Leibniz attempted to explain this in his correspondence with a French contemporary, Antoine Arnauld, in an example that compared the harmony of monadic existence to the performance of members of an orchestra or choir who,

> separately playing parts while positioned in such a way so as not to see each other or even hear each other at all, nevertheless succeed in being perfectly in harmony by simply following

their notes, each one his own, so that the one who hears them all finds there to be a marvellous harmony there . . .[81]

We could see many such examples in contemporary life, yet it is in the development of an ecology of digital memory that we come to view our prostheses and extensions in terms of an interactivity that brings monadic life – the further it refines itself – into a unity of purpose, driven by intuitive cooperation. Like Leibniz's *petites perceptions*, if you don't pay attention, the phenomena that could draw you closer to the way things are could be missed. When games developer Nintendo released a new version of its immersive body-participation gaming console, the Wii, it hinted – unsurprisingly – that what it was really selling was an idea of a new kind of collective life: inclusive, harmonious and in the moment:

> Introducing . . . Wii. As in 'we'. While the code-name 'Revolution' expressed our direction, Wii represents the answer. Wii will break down that wall that separates video game players from everybody else. Wii will put people more in touch with their games . . . and each other. But you're probably asking: What does the name mean? Wii sounds like 'we', which emphasizes this console is for everyone. Wii can easily be remembered by people around the world, no matter what language they speak. No confusion. No need to abbreviate. Just Wii. Wii has a distinctive 'ii' spelling that symbolizes both the unique controllers and the image of people gathering to play. And Wii, as a name and a console, brings something revolutionary to the world of video games that sets it apart from the crowd. So that's Wii. But now Nintendo needs you. Because, it's really not about you or me. It's about Wii. And together, Wii will change everything.[82]

The Wii, reflecting the thinking of designers whose aim was to conjure up Surf Life, was launched to the world under the banner of a slogan that undoubtedly revealed a greater truth about the times we live in than Sony, Nintendo, Apple or most observers and potential players of the game would perhaps realize:

THE WORLD HAS COME TO PLAY

It was not that the world as such had come to play the Wii that was significant about this claim, but that more generally, it contained and affirmed a wider truth about our culture and society: the world has come to – arrived at – the condition of play.

Surf Life affirms 'the now' which is often passionately engaged with what Roger Caillois described as the 'vertigo' of play, which deposits us into a condition of intuition and unconscious perception; which is is to say, forgetting. Play thus consists of

> an attempt to momentarily destroy the stability of perception and inflict a kind of voluptuous panic upon an otherwise lucid mind. In all cases, it is a question of surrendering to a kind of spasm, seizure or shock which destroys reality with sovereign brusqueness . . . various physical activities also provoke these sensations, such as the tightrope, falling or being projected into space, rapid rotation, sliding, speeding, and acceleration of vertilinear movement.[83]

There is no permanent anxiety in giving into Surf Life when it remains within one's ability to snap out of it. The attractions of this welcoming new habitat are clear: if the stresses and worries of life are always chronic, your passion for the intangible, for immanence, escapes deadly time; you defy gravity. Like spindrift, Surf Life glistens briefly in countless particles that soon enough disappear. It is not substantial, but rather here and gone. It is alive for only a short time before it evaporates into the nothingness. But we might think of it in another way, as extending the aesthetics of play into life more generally: as a million thoughts, expressed in 140 characters or less, tweet and twitter between mere mortals, countless virtual 'futures' quickly pass between financial traders, those so-called masters of the universe who until recently assumed the omniscience of ancient gods. Surf Life, in other words, has and continues to remake the world.

If the soft and hard technologies that power the new ecology of remembering and forgetting deliver us into an oblivion – an everyday of surfing that hangs on to novelty, surprise and just the simple banal 'everydayness' of having it all now – it is a condition that is mirrored in the larger socio-economic context. There the trade in financial products that are classed as derivatives (also known by names that point to an inherent intangibility, such as 'forwards', 'futures', 'swaps' and 'options') illustrates the meta-level of Surf Life. It promises – thanks in no small measure to the triumph of the computing algorithm merging to be as one with an attitude of present-mindedness as a way of life – the abolition of the future to come in favour of one that can be wildly wagered upon due to the tech-enhanced capacity to calculate the 'future' value of assets within a timeframe of seconds. It is a game of catch the wind.

If this is the real world, at some serious and meaningful objective level, then the first thing you might begin to realize, should you reflect on it, is that everything now tends towards a kind of intangibility that enjoins a new dimension of forgetting; a timeless, immemorial realm that mocks the claim memory once had on that elusive chimera we have known as self. Begin, then, at the level of the 'objective'. An invisible network channels a global trade in 'virtual' stocks and investments that reveal a contingent, precarious relationship to the actual. Such 'intangibles', though, are the tokens that permit the self-styled masters of the universe who, so to speak, hover over all other life (from their bases in Wall Street and London's Square Mile) to battle it out like the gods of Greek myth in the meta-game of contemporary life, as they attempt to channel and control the movement and intensity of the far-reaching waves on which we all ride.

In the ancient world the *mythos* functioned in a way that sought implicitly to accommodate or parry the extreme precariousness of life. The gods, like our masters of the universe, delivered favour and woe. It was an existence lived out in a permanent present, and under the impersonal forces of powers that one might appeal to, but which were distributed as a 'block of opaque powerfulness, which stood over man and opposite him, among many powers that are played off against one another, or even cancel one another out'.[84]

The dangers of an economy fuelled by virtual money were anticipated by the earliest theorists of the digital age, with Arthur Kroker and Michael Weinstein, for instance, foreseeing our current economic travails in the meeting of freely circulating information with virtual money:

> we speak of money as suddenly hyper-driven and flipped into virtual, twenty-four hour data exchanges, of the slip-streaming of consciousness . . . then we can also finally know virtual economy as a fatal, delirious, crash-event.[85]

In such times, the danger is that we may become 'celebrants of amnesia' and 'agents of forgetfulness'.[86] While it lasts, and until its dangers become apparent, however, we surf life.

CONCLUSION

The final will is that to be truly present. So that the lived moment
belongs to us and we to it and 'stay awhile' could be said to it.
Ernst Bloch

The scale of memory's domain in contemporary life is vast. In a sense
it touches on everything human – but much more. It belongs also to
times and places we have little control over, but which seem available
to us. It is disseminated through the environments, technologies and
networks that sustain us in a technologically advancing world, but
which also make forgetting characteristic of social life. Thus 'technological accomplishments', Nikolas Rose argues, 'fabricate the psychological self' and, no less, the idea of memory that has become so
central to it.[1]

The conceptual sweep required to comprehend the phenomenon
of memory would ideally move from minute particularity – smells,
sounds, images, names – to more 'global' generalizations. It would
draw from the contemporary but also from the past, and to what
our understanding of memory – and the difficulties and paradoxes
associated with it – inherits from thinkers as far back as antiquity.

Time, Kierkegaard once said, threatened always to mark us with
its passing – to write upon us every instant a new inscription.[2] It produces the kind of traces we are bound to think of in terms of memory;
which is is to say, we are marked by the experiences we have had,
and which have the potential to be recollected. Yet, as we are carried
along by the moment, the impression made by time's passing is often
something that we remain unaware of – which may be one reason
memory becomes more of a concern for those who have reached
middle age, and matters little to the young and stereotypically carefree.
Children, who remain oblivious to the traumas and upheavals that
are yet to be encountered – or which may already have left a mark

on them – have to work on memory through acts of repetition; they sing to learn and remember, just as cultures without writing once did. Before the arrival of modern techniques of storage and transmission, 'versifying' or singing, Jean-Pierre Vernant reveals, just 'meant remembering'.[3] As such, poetry and song were primary techniques of memory, and still are because they are almost primal means of impressing upon oneself something important. It is perhaps no surprise that an adult may see in the abandon and immediacy of songs that are sung by children a microcosmic glimpse of a world lost to them, but capable of making a return; an experience of the past inflected by present yearnings, disappointments, wisdom and so on.

In broader terms, it was the idea that history and society had moved from its condition of childhood innocence to disenchantment that impelled an understanding of cultural memory. In the nineteenth century, sociologists – breaking with philosophy – emerged precisely as a response to the apparent loss of traditional community, if not the idea of some primordial home. This cultural memory was an epochal phenomenon that marked modern Western societies.[4] This all helps us to make sense of the reasons a growing disquiet, which accompanies ageing, illustrates the way in which time and progress work against our ability to keep hold of the present. If memory separates us from something essentially human, its effect is demonstrated in an ethics and aesthetics of being *there* – of being, once again, at home.

It is the accumulated shocks, departures and distances travelled by a modern self-consciousness that pairs remembering most obviously with its other, forgetting. The modern human condition is to be thrust into historical time. And so we remember what is not present. We remember, or try to remember, what has been forgotten. Such efforts give an indication of how remote we can become from 'who we are', or might have been once upon a time. It implies that any attempt to ease up to the phenomenon of memory, to comprehend the reach of remembering and recollecting, must also necessarily be about the constitutive role of forgetting in it all. The fear of a forgetting that lurks in the shadows, threatening to overcome us, is a self-consciousness that necessitates the work of memory. Contemporary life therefore enacts a kind of doubling that those who were thought to move between the mythic realms of death and life might have recognized. If the forward momentum of our accelerated times induces us to metaphorically drink the waters of the Lethe, to forget and move forward, then it is no less true that the structures, habits and technologies of life today make the past something very difficult to detach or accommodate. It is in this way that memory appears as a kind of haunting or 'ghostly matter' – a thing at once embodied and incorporeal; a quality of the imagination and of the real; a thing that is both *in* time and yet assuredly destructive of time and history.[5]

The rise of memory as a subject of scholarly interest reflects no less the decline of modernity (with modernity viewed as the destroyer of pasts). At the outset of *Postmodernism; or, The Cultural Logic of Late Capitalism,* Fredric Jameson observed that if we are indeed now to be called 'postmoderns' it is because that while we are aware of the historical nature of our present position (and its seeming to unfold backwards as well as forwards) we have nonetheless 'forgotten how to think historically'.[6] Thus while history – 'the past' is maybe a more stable term in relation to memory – has seemed to stage a return in the so-called postmodern era, it does so in ways that seem to echo older ideas of memory (as collective, mythical and so on), or even as a realm of some modern variant of the immemorial (memory is absorbed by the structures of Surf Life) that modernity had seemed to vanquish in its zeal to claim the future. To forget how to think historically is thus to lose perspective on the future as much as it is to see the past as a process of development that unfolds in a forward direction that comes to be equated with an idea like 'progress'.

We might wonder, then, if memory really just acts upon us, or is sought out in various ways, in such a manner as to slow down our forward momentum, our being in time. Or perhaps it catapults us sideways into a kind of *slowness* that through a nostalgic lens, for instance, seems as if it might be drawn back towards some infinite regress. Yet, like a dream, it is always likely to recede from view just as it is about to reveal itself with the utmost clarity; a 'sticky dream' lived out in 'viscous surroundings'.[7] There are innumerable examples of how modern culture, modern men and women, have accommodated this temporal disruption – we see it in the visual arts all the time, and hear it equally in popular song. Just thinking about it provokes a recollection of a (perhaps mythical) recollection that itself evokes the lure of a time out of time. In a spare and uncluttered song titled 'Dayton, Ohio, 1913', the American songwriter Randy Newman is able to employ not only sentiment (expressed partly in the words of the song), but a tone and a tempo that knocks the real time of present experience off its axis, to suggest a longing for something lost that was contained in manners, gestures and a feeling that the world simply turned much more slowly.[8] But raking over the past in such a fashion is not to think historically. It is to revive, re-enact and in some way work through the past.

To know that memory is at once affective and psychological, socio-logical and historical – not to mention technologically mediated – suggests some of the complex ways in which it now manifests itself in our lives. But any such inventory that establishes points of reference in, say, the contemporary disciplinary categories of academic study still seems like a starting point, and seems above all to beg the question of how these *facets* of memory rub up against each other and erode, enhance or even negate the needs of memory. This is an awareness that becomes more acute given the fact that we know memory has an intimate relationship to learning, knowledge and truth – and, of course, because modern life has seen disciplinary knowledge separate such facets of memory into distinct domains of academic inquiry. Nonetheless, when we each as individuals speak to each other in everyday life about memory and experience, or about our own mem-ory of the past, we seem to know what we are referring to and probably have an implicit awareness of the dangers and absurdities of claiming ownership of something that can also seem so remote and alien. At a subjective level, we nonetheless tend to reflect back on these experi-ences we recognize as our own, and link these to memory. We need pay little attention to the fact that memory is perhaps something more puzzling and mysterious and non-human than our habits and encounters suggest. As with the air we breathe, it is not something to which we typically devote much reflection – it simply *is*, as we simply *are*.

REFERENCES

Introduction

1 Clive Thompson, 'Clive Thompson on Memory Engineering', *Wired* (27 September 2011).

2 Carolyn Kellogg, 'Scientists Write First Book in DNA', *Los Angeles Times* (20 August 2012).

3 Marcel Proust, *In Search of Lost Time*, vol. I: *Swann's Way*, trans. C. K. Scott Moncrieff and Terence Kilmartin, revd D. J. Enright (London, 1996), p. 6.

4 Novalis, *Philosophical Writings*, trans. and ed. Margaret Mahony Stoljar (Albany, NY, 1995), p. 135.

5 Friedrich Nietzsche, *Beyond Good and Evil*, trans. R. Hollingdale (London, 2003), §20, p. 50.

6 Eric L. Santner, *On Creaturely Life: Rilke, Benjamin, Sebald* (Chicago, 2006), p. 5.

7 Walter Benjamin, *The Arcades Project*, trans. Howard Eiland and Kevin McLaughlin (Cambridge, MA, 1999), p. 416.

8 Ibid., p. 471.

9 Jean-Pierre Vernant, *Myth and Thought among the Greeks*, trans. Janet Lloyd and Jeff Fort (New York, 2006), p. 435.

10 Aristotle, *Posterior Analytics*, in *The Complete Works of Aristotle: The Revised Oxford Translation*, ed. Jonathan Barnes (Princeton, NJ, 1991), vol. I, 100a, 4–9.

11 See Martin Jay, *Songs of Experience: Modern American and European Variations on a Universal Theme* (Berkeley, CA, 2006), pp. 15–16.

12 Ibid., pp. 15–16.

13 Jan Goldstein, 'Mutations of the Self', in *Biographies of Scientific Objects*, ed. Lorraine Daston (Chicago, 2000), p. 94.

14 Quoted in Sylvana Tomaselli, 'The Death and Rebirth of Character in the Eighteenth Century', in *Rewriting the Self: Histories from the Renaissance to the Present*, ed. Roy Porter (London, 1997), p. 91.

15 Jerrold Seigel, *The Idea of the Self: Thought and Experience in Western Europe since the Seventeenth Century* (Cambridge, 2005), pp. 191–2.
16 Philip Fisher, *The Vehement Passions* (Princeton, NJ, 2003), p. 44.
17 Ibid.
18 See the story of 'EP' in Joshua Foer, 'Remember This: In the Archives of the Brain', *National Geographic* (November 2007), pp. 32–57.
19 Aristotle, *On Memory*, in *The Complete Works of Aristotle, The Revised Oxford Translation*, ed. Jonathan Barnes (Princeton, NJ, 1991), vol. I, 449b24–449b30.
20 Ian Hacking, *Rewriting the Soul: Multiple Personality and the Sciences of Memory* (Princeton, NJ, 1995), pp. 199–201.
21 Matthew Rampley, *Nietzsche, Aesthetics and Modernity* (Cambridge, 2000), p. 140.
22 Vernant, *Myth and Thought among the Greeks*, p. 122.
23 Ibid.
24 Paul Ricoeur, *Memory, History, Forgetting*, trans. Kathleen Blamey and David Pellauer (Chicago, 2004), p. 284.
25 Matt K. Matsuda, *The Memory of the Modern* (New York and London, 1996), p. vi.
26 Kerwin Lee Klein, 'On the Emergence of *Memory* in Historical Discourse', *Representations*, 69, Special Issue: 'Grounds for Remembering' (2006), p. 129.

1 Pasts

1 Robert Pogue Harrison, *The Dominion of the Dead* (Chicago, 2003), p. xi.
2 Ibid.
3 Martin Heidegger, *Being and Time*, trans. John Macquarrie and Edward Robinson (Oxford, 1962), §329, p. 377.
4 Martin Heidegger, *The Fundamental Concepts of Metaphysics: World, Finitude, Solitude*, trans. William McNeill and Nicholas Walker (Bloomington, IN, 2001), p. 6; Novalis, *Philosophical Writings*, trans. and ed. Margaret Mahony Stoljar (Albany, NY, 1997), p. 135.
5 Martin Heidegger, *Early Greek Thinking*, trans. D. F. Krell and A. F. Capuzzi (New York, 1984), p. 108.
6 Friedrich Nietzsche, *Beyond Good and Evil*, trans. R. Hollingdale (London, 2003), §20, p. 50.
7 Fredric Jameson, *The Seeds of Time* (New York, 1994), p. 84.
8 The quotation is from Heidegger, *Early Greek Thinking*, p. 108.
9 The recollection of divine memory is anamnesis which, according to Angus Nicholls and Martin Leibscher, *Thinking the Unconscious: Nineteenth-century Germàn Thought* (Cambridge, 2010), may be

thought of as an early variant of 'the unconscious', see p. 4.

10 In myth, memory is anamnesis – this is what pre-dates philosophy. See also Eric Voeglin, *Order and History* (Columbia, MI, 2001).

11 Edith Hall, *The Return of Ulysses: A Cultural History of Homer's Odyssey* (London, 2008), p. 164.

12 Homer, *The Odyssey*, trans. E. V. Rieu and D.C.H. Rieu (London, 1991), p. 72, Book 5, ll. 8off.

13 See Theodor Adorno and Max Horkheimer, *Dialectic of Enlightenment*, trans. John Cumming (London, 1997); J. M. Bernstein, *Adorno: Disenchantment and Ethics* (Cambridge, 2001), p. 76.

14 For a short critical appraisal of the *Dialectic of Enlightenment* and its implications for an understanding of modernity, see Robert B. Pippin, *Modernism as a Philosophical Problem* (Oxford, 1999), pp. 164–5.

15 It is worth pointing out that Homer tells us about memory in other ways: there are descriptions of feats of memory, and so on. But what is crucial here is the existential fate of a mythical individual as a reflection of our own modern condition.

16 Svetlana Boym, *The Future of Nostalgia* (New York, 2001), p. 13.

17 Adorno and Horkheimer, *Dialectic of Enlightenment*, p. 58.

18 Peter Sloterdijk, *Spheres*, vol. I: *Bubbles*, trans. Wieland Hoban (Los Angeles, CA, 2011), p. 487.

19 Ibid., p. 275.

20 Homer, *The Odyssey*, p. 184, Book 12, ll. 190–95.

21 Bernstein, *Adorno*, p. 87.

22 Hans Blumenberg, *Work on Myth*, trans. Robert M. Wallace (Cambridge, MA, 1985), p. 8.

23 Adorno and Horkheimer, *Dialectic of Enlightenment*, p. 32.

24 Ibid., p. 46.

25 Harvie Ferguson, *Self-identity and Everyday Life* (London, 2009), pp. 71, 69.

26 Jean-Luc Nancy, *Hegel: The Restlessness of the Negative*, trans. Jason Smith and Steven Miller (Minneapolis, MN, 2002), p. 3.

27 G.W.F. Hegel, *Phenomenology of Spirit*, trans. A. V. Miller (Oxford, 1977), p. 217.

28 Ibid., p. 19.

29 Ernst Bloch, *The Principle of Hope*, trans. N. Plaice et al. (Cambridge, MA, 1986), vol. I, p. 139.

30 Quoted ibid.

31 See the discussion in Boym, *The Future of Nostalgia*, p. 24.

32 In Karl Marx, *Grundrisse: Foundations of the Critique of Political Economy* (London, 1993), p. 111.

33 Nancy, *Hegel*, p. 17.

34 Marshall Berman, *All That Is Solid Melts Into Air: The Experience of Modernity* (London, 1983), p. 15.

35 See, for example, Peter Fritzsche, *Stranded in the Present: Modern Time and the Melancholy of History* (Harvard, MA, 2004)

36 See Homer, *The Odyssey*, p. 76, Book 5, ll. 203–24.

37 Jean-Pierre Vernant, *Myth and Thought among the Greeks*, trans. Janet Lloyd and Jeff Fort (New York, 2006), p. 121.

38 See Jean-Pierre Vernant, *Myth and Society in Ancient Greece*, trans. Janet Lloyd (New York, 1988); and Blumenberg, *Work on Myth*.

39 Vernant, *Myth and Thought among the Greeks*, p. 121.

40 See, for example, J. A. Barash, 'The Sources of Memory', *Journal of the History of Ideas*, LVIII/4 (October 1997), pp. 707–17.

41 Hans Blumenberg, *The Legitimacy of the Modern Age*, trans. Robert M. Wallace (Cambridge, MA, 1983), p. 116.

42 Ibid., p. 146.

43 R. G. Collingwood, *The Idea of History* [1946] (Oxford, 1961), p. 78.

44 Joseph Levine, *The Autonomy of History: Truth and Method from Erasmus to Gibbon* (Chicago, 1999), p. 160.

45 F. R. Ankersmit, *Sublime Historical Experience* (Stanford, CA, 2005), p. 365.

46 F. R. Ankersmit, *History and Tropology: The Rise and Fall of Metaphor* (Berkeley, CA, 1994), p. 16.

47 Ankersmit, *Sublime Historical Experience*, p. 365

48 Ankersmit, *History and Tropology*, p. 16.

49 Quoted in Neville Morley, *Antiquity and Modernity* (Oxford, 2009), pp. 120–21.

50 I am mindful of Jacques Le Goff's assertion that 'it is not easy to talk about history', especially so within the confines of this particular study, whose focus is both more scattered in its pursuit of aspects of the phenomena of memory, and more restricted in its length. As well as Jacques Le Goff, *History and Memory*, trans. Steven Rendall and Elizabeth Claman (New York, 1992), a more thoroughgoing and authoritative account of history's relationship to memory can be found in Paul Ricoeur, *Memory, History, Forgetting*, trans. Kathleen Blamey and David Pellauer (Chicago, 2004).

51 Pierre Nora, 'Between Memory and History: *Les Lieux de mémoire*', trans. Marc Roudebush, *Representations*, XXVI (1989), pp. 7–25.

52 See Ricoeur, *Memory, History, Forgetting*, p. 241.

53 Berman, *All That Is Solid Melts Into Air*, p. 17.

54 Roy Porter, *Enlightenment: Britain and the Creation of the Modern World* (London, 2000), p. 57.

55 Collingwood, *The Idea of History*, p. 234.

56 Ibid., p. 235.

57 Ibid., p. 58.
58 See E. H. Carr, *What Is History?* (Harmondsworth, 1964), pp. 21–2.
59 The word 'history' is related to 'the Sanskrit *vettas*, witness, and the
     Greek *istor*, a witness in the sense of "one who sees"'. See Le Goff,
     History and Memory, p. 101–2.
60 Ankersmit, *History and Tropology*, p. 121.
61 Collingwood, *The Idea of History*, pp. 282–3.
62 Carr, *What Is History?* p. 26.
63 Arthur C. Danto, 'Historical Understanding and the Problem of
     Other Periods', *Journal of Philosophy*, LXIII (1966), p. 566.
64 Le Goff, *History and Memory*, p. 111.
65 David Lowenthal, *The Past is a Foreign Country* (Cambridge, 1985),
     p. 187.
66 See Nora, 'Between Memory and History'.
67 Simon Schama, *Landscape and Memory* (London, 1995), p. 621.
68 Carlo Ginzburg, 'Distance and Perspective: Two Metaphors', in
     Wooden Eyes: Nine Reflections on Distance, trans. Martin Ryle and
     Kate Soper (New York, 2001), p. 153. For more on the Leibniz
     connection, see Hanna Salumi, 'Cultural History, the Possible, and
     the Principle of Plenitude', *History and Theory*, L (2011), pp. 171–87.
69 Carlo Ginzburg, *Clues, Myths and the Historical Method*, trans. John
     and Ann C. Tedeschi (Baltimore, MD, 1989), pp. 101–2.
70 Ibid., p. 115.
71 Ibid.
72 Ankersmit, *History and Tropology*, p. 122. The emphasis on 'attribution'
     here is mine.
73 Carlo Ginzburg, *The Cheese and the Worms: The Cosmos of a
     Sixteenth-century Miller*, trans John and Ann C. Tedeschi (Baltimore,
     MD, 1992), p. xiv.
74 Ibid., p. xv.
75 Ibid., p. xi.
76 Ibid., p. 6.
77 Ibid., p. xi.
78 Ibid., p. xii.
79 Ankersmit, *History and Tropology*, pp. 122, 123.
80 Ibid., pp. 122.
81 On Duchamp's readymades as an expression of the unconscious in
     conceptual art, see my discussion of the subject in John Scanlan,
     'Duchamp's Wager: Disguise, the Play of Surface, and Disorder',
     History of the Human Sciences, XVI/3 (2003), pp. 1–20.
82 The quote here is from Ginzburg's discussion of the similarities
     between his and Freud's methods in Ginzburg, *Clues, Myths and the
     Historical Method*, p. 101. The approach taken by microhistory is also

explored and defended in several other places: the two Prefaces in Ginzburg, *The Cheese and the Worms*; the essay I have been quoting from, 'Clues: Roots of an Evidential Paradigm', in Ginzburg, *Clues, Myths and the Historical Method*, pp. 96–125; and a more recent essay by Ginzburg, 'Minutiae, Close-up, Microanalysis', *Critical Inquiry*, XXXIV/1 (Autumn 2007), pp. 174–89.

83 See Ricoeur, *Memory, History, Forgetting*, p. 214.
84 Leibniz, from the 'Monadology' (§57), quoted in Ginzburg, 'Distance and Perspective: Two Metaphors', p. 152.
85 Ginzburg, 'Minutiae, Close-up, Microanalysis', p. 187.
86 Ibid., p. 179.
87 Friedrich Nietzsche, *Untimely Meditations*, trans. R. Hollingdale (Cambridge, 1997), p. 78.
88 Lowenthal, *The Past is a Foreign Country*, p. 20.
89 Matthew Rampley, *Nietzsche, Aesthetics and Modernity* (Cambridge, 2000), p. 139.
90 Nietzsche, *Untimely Meditations*, p. 64.
91 Rosemary Sweet, *Antiquaries: The Discovery of the Past in Eighteenth-century Britain* (London, 2004), pp. 2–3.
92 Nietzsche, *Untimely Meditations*, p. 74.
93 Schama, *Landscape and Memory*, p. 16.
94 Raphael Samuel, *Theatres of Memory*, vol. I: *Past and Present in Contemporary Culture* (London, 1994), p. 208.
95 Ibid., p. 221.
96 Ibid., p. 208.
97 Ibid., p. 205.
98 Nora, 'Between Memory and History'.
99 Ibid., p. 12.
100 Tim Edensor, 'The Ghosts of Industrial Ruins: Ordering and Disordering Memory in Excessive Space', *Environment and Planning D: Society and Space*, XXIII (2005), pp. 829–49.
101 M. Christine Boyer, *The City of Collective Memory: Its Historical Imagery and Architectural Entertainments* (Cambridge, MA, 1994), p. 54.
102 See David Lowenthal, *The Heritage Crusade and the Spoils of History* (Cambridge, 1998).
103 On the interplay of fact and fiction in Sebald's books, see Lynne Sharon Schwartz, ed., *The Emergence of Memory: Conversations with W. G. Sebald* (New York, 2007).
104 W. G. Sebald, *The Emigrants*, trans. Michael Hulse (London, 2002), pp. 168–9.
105 The quotes are from Friedrich Nietzsche, 'On the Genealogy of Morality: A Polemic', in *The Nietzsche Reader*, ed. Keith Ansell

Pearson and Duncan Large (Oxford, 2006), p. 408.

106 Sloterdijk, *Bubbles*, p. 19.

107 Ibid., p. 28.

108 Friedrich Kittler, *Gramophone, Film, Typewriter*, trans. Geoffrey Winthrop-Young and Michael Wutz (Stanford, CA, 1999), p. 81.

109 Walter Benjamin, *Walter Benjamin's Archive*, ed. Ursula Marx et al., trans. Esther Leslie (London and New York, 2007), p. 49.

110 Ibid., p. 52.

111 Walter Benjamin, 'A Berlin Childhood Around 1900', in *Selected Writings*, vol. III: *1935–1938*, trans. Edmund Jephcott, Howard Eiland et al. (Cambridge, MA, 2002), pp. 385–6.

112 Ibid., p. 350.

113 Siegfried Kracauer, 'On the Writings of Walter Benjamin', in *The Mass Ornament: Weimar Essays*, trans. Thomas Y. Levin (Cambridge, MA, 1995), p. 262.

114 Walter Benjamin, 'Old Toys', in *Selected Writings*, vol. II, Part 1: *1927–1930*, trans. Rodney Livingstone et al. (Cambridge, MA, 1999), p. 100.

115 Walter Benjamin, 'The Cultural History of Toys', in *Selected Writings*, vol. II, Part 1: *1927–1930*, p. 115.

116 I allude here to Benjamin's recollection of his grandmother's home producing in him 'immemorial feelings of bourgeois security'. See 'A Berlin Childhood Around 1900', p. 369.

117 Walter Benjamin, 'One-way Street', in *One-way Street and Other Writings*, trans. Edmund Jephcott and Kingsley Shorter (London, 1997), p. 75.

118 Ibid.

119 Benjamin, 'A Berlin Childhood Around 1900', p. 344.

120 Susan Buck-Morss, *The Dialectics of Seeing: Walter Benjamin and the Arcades Project* (Cambridge, MA, 1991), p. 261.

121 Ibid., p. 268.

122 Ibid., p. 273.

123 Ludwig Wittgenstein, *Philosophical Investigations*, 3rd edn, trans. G.E.M. Anscombe (Oxford, 1967), p. 157.

124 Buck-Morss, *The Dialectics of Seeing*, p. 39. Buck-Morss discusses the importance of 'childhood cognition' to Benjamin's thought, and to the Arcades Project, on pp. 261–6.

125 Harry Harootunian, *History's Disquiet: Modernity, Cultural Practice, and the Question of Everyday Life* (New York, 2000), p. 18.

126 For a short introduction to the debates, see Phil Mollon, *Freud and False Memory Syndrome* (Cambridge and New York, 2000).

127 Sigmund Freud, 'Remembering, Repeating and Working Through', in *The Standard Edition of the Complete Psychological Works*, trans. J. Strachey (London, 1955), vol. VI, pp. 274–5.

128 Walter Benjamin, 'Excavation and Memory', in *Selected Writings*, vol. II, Part 2: *1931–1934* (Cambridge, MA, 1999), p. 576.

129 See Sarah Ley Roff, 'Benjamin and Psychoanalysis', in *The Cambridge Companion to Benjamin*, ed. David S. Ferris (Cambridge, 2006), pp. 115–33.

130 Benjamin, *The Arcades Project*, p. 372.

131 Kracauer, 'On the Writings of Walter Benjamin', p. 262.

132 Christine Buci-Glucksmann, *Baroque Reason: The Aesthetics of Modernity*, trans. Patrick Camiller (London, Thousand Oaks, CA, and New Delhi, 1994), p. 45.

133 Antoine Compagnon, *The Five Paradoxes of Modernity*, trans. Franklin Philip (New York, 1994), p. 16.

134 Buck-Morss, *The Dialectics of Seeing*, p. x.

135 Walter Benjamin, 'The Storyteller', in *Illuminations*, trans. Harry H. Zohn (London, 1994), pp. 93–4.

136 Eric L. Santner, *On Creaturely Life: Rilke, Benjamin, Sebald* (Chicago, 2006), p. 17.

137 Benjamin, *Walter Benjamin's Archive*, p. 59.

138 Gershom Scholem, *Walter Benjamin: The Story of a Friendship* (New York, 2003), p. 47.

11 Presences

1 Walter Benjamin, 'On Some Motifs in Baudelaire', in *Illuminations*, trans. Harry H. Zohn (London, 1994), pp. 157.

2 Paul Ricoeur, *Memory, History, Forgetting*, trans. Kathleen Blamey and David Pellauer (Chicago, 2004), p. 5.

3 Ibid., p. xvi.

4 Henri Bergson, *Matter and Memory*, trans. N. M. Paul and W. S. Palmer (New York, 1991), p. 145.

5 Friedrich Kittler, *Optical Media* (Cambridge, 2010), p. 35.

6 Ibid.

7 Martin Jay, *Downcast Eyes: The Denigration of Vision in Twentieth-century French Thought* (Berkeley, CA, 1993), pp. 198–9.

8 Ibid., p. 199.

9 Eduardo Cadava, *Words of Light: Theses on the Photography of History* (Princeton, NJ, 1997), p. 91.

10 Henri Bergson, *Matter and Memory*, trans. N. M. Paul and W. S. Palmer (Mineola, NY, 2004), pp. 24–5.

11 Marcel Proust, *In Search of Lost Time*, vol. I: *Swann's Way*, trans. C. K. Scott Moncrieff and Terence Kilmartin, revd D. J. Enright (London, 1996).

12 Joshua Landy, *Philosophy as Fiction: Self, Deception and Knowledge*

in Proust (Oxford, 2004), p. 9.

13 M. H. Abrams, *The Mirror and the Lamp: Romantic Theory and the Critical Tradition* (Oxford, 1971), p. 57.

14 John Locke, *Essay Concerning Human Understanding*, abridged and ed. with an introduction by John W. Yolton (London, 1976), p. 76.

15 Jay, *Downcast Eyes*, p. 85.

16 Anne Friedberg, *The Virtual Window: From Alberti to Microsoft* (Cambridge, MA, 2009), p. 51.

17 Marina Warner, *Fantastic Metamorphoses, Other Worlds* (Oxford, 2002), p. 171.

18 René Descartes, *A Discourse on Method: Meditations and Principles*, trans. John Veitch (London and Melbourne, 1986), p. 84.

19 Ibid., p. 85.

20 Daniel Pick, 'Stories of the Eye', in *Rewriting the Self: Histories from the Renaissance to the Present*, ed. Roy Porter (London, 1997), p. 188.

21 Ibid.

22 Jorge Luis Borges, 'Funes, His Memory', in *Fictions*, trans. Andrew Hurley (London, 2000), p. 96.

23 Pick, 'Stories of the Eye', p. 188.

24 John Berger, *The Camerawork Essays: Context and Meaning in Photography*, ed. Jessica Evans (London, 1997), p. 45.

25 Ibid.

26 Ibid.

27 See, for example, Maurice Halbwachs, *On Collective Memory*, ed. and trans. with an introduction by Lewis A. Coser (Chicago and London, 1992).

28 Darren Tofts, *Memory Trade: A Prehistory of Cyberculture*, illus. Murray McKeich (North Ryde, 1998), p. 66.

29 Gilles Deleuze, *Foucault*, trans. Seán Hand (Minneapolis, MN, 1988), pp. 107–8.

30 Evans Lansing Smith, *The Hero Journey in Literature: Parables of Poesis* (Lanham, MD, 1997), p. 42.

31 See, for instance, Sigmund Freud, 'Preface to Reik's *Ritual: Psychoanalytic Studies*', in *The Standard Edition of the Complete Psychological Works*, trans. J. Strachey (London, 1955), vol. XVII, p. 260.

32 Erwin Rohde, *Psyche: The Cult of Souls and Belief in Immortality Among the Greeks*, trans. from the 8th edn by W. B. Hillis (London, 1925), p. 5.

33 Ibid.

34 W. G. Sebald, quoted in Eleanor Wachtel, 'The Ghost Hunter', in *The Emergence of Memory: Conversations with W. G. Sebald*, ed. Lynne Sharon Schwartz (New York, 2007), p. 40.

35 David Lenson, *On Drugs* (Minneapolis, MN, 2005), pp. 95–6.

36 Hillel Schwartz, *The Culture of the Copy: Striking Likenesses, Unreasonable Facsimiles* (New York, 1996), p. 362.

37 Jacques Derrida, *Points . . . Interviews, 1974–1994*, trans. Peggy Kamuf et al. (Stanford, CA, 1995), pp. 235–6.

38 Marianne Hirsch, 'Projected Memory: Holocaust Photographs in Personal and Public Fantasy', in *Acts of Memory: Cultural Recall in the Present*, ed. Mieke Bal, Jonathan Crewe and Leo Spitzer (Hanover, NH, 1999), pp. 8–9.

39 Pierre Nora, 'General Introduction: Between Memory and History', in *Realms of Memory: Rethinking the French Past*, trans. Arthur Goldhammer (New York, 1996), vol. I, pp. 6, 8.

40 Ibid., p. 8.

41 Ibid., p. 9.

42 See Robert Pippin, *The Persistence of Subjectivity: On the Kantian Aftermath* (Cambridge, 2005), p. 318.

43 Quoted in Chitra Ramalingam, 'Fixing Transience: Photography and Other Images of Time in 1830s London', in *Time and Photography*, ed. Jan Baetens, Alexander Streitberger and Hilde Van Gelder (Leuven, 2010), p. 16.

44 Susan Sontag, *On Photography* (London, 1978), p. 18.

45 Warner, *Fantastic Metamorphoses, Other Worlds*, p. 163.

46 Jay, *Downcast Eyes*, p. 124.

47 Benjamin, 'On Some Motifs in Baudelaire', pp. 170–71. Also Siegfried Kracauer, as quoted in David Frisby, *Cityscapes of Modernity* (Oxford, 2001), p. 49: 'The Paris crowds omnipresent in Baudelaire's *Les Fleurs du mal* function as stimuli which call forth irritating kaleidoscopic sensations.'

48 Elissa Marder, *Dead Time: Temporal Orders in the Wake of Modernity* (Stanford, CA, 2001), pp. 2–3.

49 Pippin, *The Persistence of Subjectivity*, p. 318.

50 Benjamin, 'On Some Motifs in Baudelaire', p. 156.

51 Christoph Asendorf, *Batteries of Life: On the History of Things and Their Perception in Modernity*, trans. Don Reneau (Berkeley, CA, 1993), p. 83.

52 Ibid.

53 Roland Barthes, *Camera Lucida*, trans. Richard Howard (London, 1993), p. 4.

54 Asendorf, *Batteries of Life*, p. 83.

55 Sontag, *On Photography*, p. 87.

56 Ibid., p. 15.

57 Barthes, *Camera Lucida*, p. 77.

58 Raphael Samuel, *Theatres of Memory*, vol. I: *Past and Present in Contemporary Culture* (London, 1994), p. 315.

59 Walter Benjamin, 'The Work of Art in the Age of Mechanical Reproduction', in *Illuminations*, p. 219.

60 Esther Leslie, 'Absent-minded Professors: Etch-a-sketching Academic Forgetting', in *Regimes of Memory*, ed. Susannah Radstone and Katharine Hodgkin (London, 2003), p. 177.

61 Quoted in Giorgio Agamben, *Potentialities: Collected Essays in Philosophy*, trans. Daniel Heller-Roazen (Stanford, CA, 1999), p. 158.

62 Barthes, *Camera Lucida*, p. 85.

63 Roland Barthes, *Roland Barthes* (Berkeley, CA, 1994), p. 36.

64 Barthes, *Camera Lucida*, p. 92.

65 Benjamin, 'The Work of Art in the Age of Mechanical Reproduction', p. 230.

66 Philippe Garner, 'Fleeting Images: Photographers, Models and the Media – London, 1966', in *Antonioni's Blow-up*, ed. Philippe Garner and David Alan Mellor (Göttingen, 2010), p. 117.

67 William C. Pamerleau, *Existentialist Cinema* (Basingstoke, 2009), p. 85.

68 Ibid.

69 Barbara Wright, 'Baudelaire's Poetic Journey in *Les Fleurs du Mal*', in *The Cambridge Companion to Baudelaire*, ed. Rosemary Lloyd (Cambridge, 2005), p. 48. See also Charles Baudelaire, 'The Modern Public and Photography', in *Classic Essays in Photography*, ed. Alan Trachtenberg (New Haven, CT, 1980).

70 Baudelaire, quoted in Jay, *Downcast Eyes*, p. 83.

71 Siegfried Zielinski, *Deep Time of the Media: Towards an Archaeology of Hearing and Seeing by Technical Means* (Cambridge, MA, 2006), p. 31.

72 Benjamin, 'The Work of Art in the Age of Mechanical Reproduction', p. 229.

73 Mary Poovey, *A History of the Modern Fact* (Chicago, 1998), p. 255.

74 Ibid.

75 Aleida Assmann, 'Texts, Traces, Trash: The Changing Media of Cultural Memory', *Representations*, LVI (Autumn 1996), p. 131.

76 Michael Löwy, *Fire Alarm: Reading Walter Benjamin's 'On the Concept of History'*, trans. Chris Turner (London and New York, 2005), p. 31.

77 Quoted ibid., pp. 29–30.

78 Emily Thompson, *The Soundscape of Modernity: Architectural Acoustics and the Culture of Listening in America, 1900–1933* (Cambridge, MA, 2002), p. 12; Kittler, *Gramophone, Film, Typewriter* (Stanford, CA, 1999), p. 94.

79 Jonathan Sterne, 'The Preservation of Paradox in Digital Audio', in *Sound Souvenirs and Audio Memory*, ed. Karen Bijsterveld and José

van Dijck (Amsterdam, 2009), p. 57.

80 See the section titled 'Gramophone', in Kittler, *Gramophone, Film, Typewriter,* pp. 21–114.

81 Kittler, *Gramophone, Film, Typewriter*, p. 86.

82 Frances A. Yates, *The Art of Memory* (London, 2002), p. 31.

83 Ibid., p. 18.

84 Ibid.

85 Quintilian, *The Orator's Education (Books 11–12)*, ed. and trans. Donald A. Russell (Cambridge, MA, 2001), p. 67.

86 Ibid.

87 Mary Carruthers, *The Book of Memory: A Study of Memory in Medieval Culture* (Cambridge, 2008), p. 93.

88 Walter Benjamin, 'The Storyteller', in *Illuminations*, pp. 93–4.

89 Thompson, *The Soundscape of Modernity*, p. 1.

90 Ibid., pp. 233–4.

91 Michel Serres and Bruno Latour, *Conversations on Science, Culture and Time* (Ann Arbor, MI, 1995), p. 60.

92 Alain Corbin, *Village Bells: Sound and Meaning in the 19th-century French Countryside* (London, 1999), pp. 96–7.

93 Brandon LaBelle, *Background Noise: Perspectives on Sound Art* (London, 2006), p. 24.

94 Plato, *Phaedrus*, trans. Robert Waterfield (Oxford, 2002), §275a, p. 69.

95 Jacques Derrida, 'Plato's Pharmacy', in *Dissemination*, trans. Barbara Johnson (London and New York, 2004), p. 76.

96 Ibid.

97 Derrida, *Points*, p. 234.

98 Derrida, 'Plato's Pharmacy', p. 78.

99 Assmann, 'Texts, Traces, Trash', p. 124.

100 Ibid., p. 123.

101 Lisa Gitelman, *Always Already New: Media, History and the Data of Culture* (Cambridge, MA, 2006), pp. 18–19.

102 Walter Benjamin, 'A Small History of Photography', in *One-way Street and Other Writings*, trans. Edmund Jephcott and Kingsley Shorter (London, 1997), p. 243.

103 Kittler, *Gramophone, Film, Typewriter*, p. 89.

104 Gerhard Richter, *Benjamin's Ghosts: Interventions in Contemporary Literary and Cultural Theory* (Stanford, CA, 2002), p. 66.

105 David Toop, *Haunted Weather: Music, Silence and Memory* (London, 2004), p. 42.

106 Douglas Kahn, *Noise, Water, Meat: A History of Sound in the Arts* (Cambridge, MA, 1999), p. 4.

107 N. Katherine Hayles, 'Voices Out of Bodies, Bodies Out of Voices: Audiotape and the Production of Subjectivity', in *Sound States:*

Innovative Poetics and Acoustical Technologies, ed. Adalaide Morris (Chapel Hill, NC, 1997), p. 77.

108 LaBelle, *Background Noise*, p. 27.

109 Walter Benjamin, *The Arcades Project*, trans. Howard Eiland and Kevin McLaughlin (Cambridge, MA, 1999).

110 Hayles, 'Voices Out of Bodies, Bodies Out of Voices', p. 77.

111 See, for instance, Thomas B. Holmes, *Electronic and Experimental Music: Pioneers in Technology and Composition* (London, 2002), pp. 77–84.

112 LaBelle, *Background Noise*, p. 25.

113 George Steiner, *Grammars of Creation* (London, 2002), p. 275.

114 Tim Hodgkinson, 'An Interview with Pierre Schaeffer', in *The Book of Music and Nature: An Anthology of Sounds, Words, Thoughts*, ed. David Rothenberg and Marta Ulvaeus (Middleton, CT, 2001), p. 34.

115 Eduardo de la Fuente, *Twentieth-century Music and the Sociology of Modern Culture* (London, 2009), p. 145.

116 Sumanth Gopinath, 'The Problem of the Political in Steve Reich's Come Out', in *Sound Commitments: Avant-garde Music and the Sixties*, ed. Robert Adlington (Oxford, 2009), p. 123.

117 Ben Highmore, *Everyday Life and Cultural Theory* (London and New York, 2002), p. 61.

118 Benjamin, *The Arcades Project*, p. 469.

119 Ibid., p. 464.

120 John May and Nigel Thrift, *TimeSpace: Geographies of Temporality* (London, 2004), p. 261

121 Jean-Pierre Vernant, *Myth and Thought among the Greeks*, trans. Janet Lloyd and Jeff Fort (New York, 2006), p. 121.

122 Quoted in Marina Warner, *Phantasmagoria: Spirit Visions, Metaphors, and Media into the Twenty-first Century* (Oxford, 2006).

123 David Byrne, 'Bush of Ghosts: Making Of' (2005), http://bushofghosts.wmg.com, accessed 14 August 2010.

124 Michel Serres, *Genesis*, trans. Genevieve James and James Nielson (Ann Arbor, MI, 1995), p. 14.

125 Ibid., p. 71.

126 John McCole, *Walter Benjamin and the Antinomies of Tradition* (Ithaca, NY, 1993), p. 262.

127 Fredric Jameson, 'The End of Temporality', *Critical Inquiry*, XXIX/4 (2003), p. 712.

128 Harvie Ferguson, *Self-identity and Everyday Life* (London, 2009), pp. 153–90.

129 Jameson, 'The End of Temporality', p. 713; Ferguson, *Self-identity and Everyday Life*, p. 164.

130 Jonathan Crary, *Suspensions of Perception: Attention, Spectacle*,

and Modern Culture (Cambridge, MA, 1999), pp. 31–2.

131 Michael Bull, 'The Auditory Nostalgia of iPod Culture', in *Sound Souvenirs and Audio Memory*, ed. Karen Bijsterveld and José van Dijck (Amsterdam, 2009), p. 83.

132 Tom Leonard, '"iPod Oblivion" Set to Become Illegal in New York', *Daily Telegraph* (8 February 2007), available at www.telegraph.co.uk.

133 Leander Kahney, *Cult of iPod* (San Francisco, CA, 2005), p. 20.

134 Ibid.

135 Ferguson, *Self-identity and Everyday Life*, p. 165.

136 Jameson, 'The End of Temporality', p. 712.

137 Ibid.

138 Ferguson, *Self-identity and Everyday Life*, p. 165.

III Ecologies

1 Raphael Samuel, *Theatres of Memory*, vol. I: *Past and Present in Contemporary Culture* (London, 1994), p. 218.

2 David Adams Leeming, *Mythology: The Voyage of the Hero* (Oxford, 1998), p. 5.

3 Mircea Eliade, *Myth and Reality*, trans. Willard R. Trask (New York and Evanston, IL, 1963), p. 123.

4 Hannu Salmi, 'Cultural History, the Possible and the Principle of Plenitude', *History and Theory*, L (May 2011), p. 175.

5 Jonathan Flatley, *Affective Mapping: Melancholia and the Politics of Modernism* (Cambridge, MA, 2008), p. 28.

6 See Fredric Jameson, *The Seeds of Time* (New York, 1994), p. 84.

7 E. P. Thompson, 'Time, Work-discipline and Industrial Capitalism', *Past and Present*, XXXVIII (1967), p. 73.

8 Jameson, *The Seeds of Time*, p. 84.

9 Emile Durkheim, *The Elementary Forms of Religious Life*, trans. John Ward Swain (New York, 2008), p. 427.

10 Ibid., p. 375.

11 Jerrold Seigel, *The Idea of the Self: Thought and Experience in Western Europe since the Seventeenth Century* (Cambridge, 2005), p. 21.

12 The contrast with Aby Warburg is made in Jan Assmann, 'Collective Memory and Cultural Identity', *New German Critique*, LXV (Spring/Summer 1995), pp. 125–33.

13 Peter Krapp, *Déjà Vu: Aberrations of Cultural Memory* (Minneapolis, MN, 2004), p. xxix.

14 Maurice Halbwachs, *On Collective Memory*, trans. Lewis A. Coser (Chicago, 1992), p. 52.

15 Seigel, *The Idea of the Self*, p. 518; quote p. 522.

16 Halbwachs, *On Collective Memory*, p. 37.

17 Ibid.
18 Gianni Vattimo, *The Transparent Society* (Cambridge, 1992), p. 29.
19 Leeming, *Mythology*, p. 6.
20 Halbwachs, *On Collective Memory*, p. 37.
21 Assmann, 'Collective Memory and Cultural Identity', p. 127.
22 Jan Assmann, *Moses the Egyptian: The Memory of Egypt in Western Monotheism* (Cambridge, 1997), p. 14.
23 Halbwachs, *On Collective Memory*, p. 51.
24 Maurice Halbwachs, *The Collective Memory*, trans. Francis J. Ditter Jr and Vida Yazdi Ditter (New York, 1980), pp. 85–6.
25 Ibid., p. 131.
26 See the essays in Karin Tilmans, Frank Van Vree and Jay Winter, eds, *Performing the Past: Memory, History and Identity in Modern Europe* (Amsterdam, 2010).
27 Henry McDonald, 'Petrol Bombs Thrown in Belfast during Second Night of Rioting', *The Guardian* (27 October 2010); 'Loyalists Say "Provocative" Police Tactics Sparked Riots in Belfast', *The Guardian* (26 October 2010). The Historical Enquiries Team was investigating some 1,800 unsolved murders as part of the reconciliation process, and found it difficult to dissociate itself from the Police. One member of a paramilitary group interviewed in the *Guardian* article revealed the difficulties the process was causing when he said that: 'It is impossible to convince people to move on . . . if the police are still arresting them for things that occurred in the past, things that we were meant to leave behind.'
28 The background to the emergence of this reconciliation process in Northern Ireland is described in Maria Duffy, *Paul Ricoeur's Pedagogy of Pardon: A Narrative Theory of Memory and Forgetting* (New York, 2009), pp. 1–10.
29 Giorgio Agamben, 'The Tradition of the Immemorial', in *Potentialities: Collected Essays in Philosophy*, trans. Daniel Heller-Roazen (Stanford, CA, 2000), pp. 104–15.
30 Ibid., p. 104.
31 Ibid., pp. 104–15.
32 Friedrich Nietzsche, 'On the Genealogy of Morality: A Polemic', in *The Nietzsche Reader*, ed. Keith Ansell Pearson and Duncan Large (Oxford, 2006), p. 410.
33 Cathy Caruth, 'Introduction', in *Trauma: Explorations in Memory*, ed. C. Caruth (Baltimore, MD, 1995), p. 8.
34 Sigmund Freud, 'Remembering, Repeating and Working Through', in *The Standard Edition of the Complete Psychological Works*, trans. J. Strachey (London, 1955), vol. VI, p. 148.
35 Jean-Pierre Vernant, *Myth and Thought among the Greeks*, trans.

Janet Lloyd and Jeff Fort (New York, 2006), p. 121.

36 Gregg Lambert, *The Return of the Baroque in Modern Culture* (New York, 2004), p. 70.

37 See, for example, Ana Lucia Araujo, *Public Memory of Slavery: Victims and Perpetrators in the South Atlantic* (Amherst, NY, and London, 2010)

38 Gilles Deleuze and Félix Guattari, *A Thousand Plateaus: Capitalism and Schizophrenia*, trans. Brian Massumi (London and Minneapolis, MN, 1987), p. 266.

39 Marc Augé, *Non-places: Introduction to an Anthropology of Supermodernity*, trans. John Howe (London, 1995), p. 86.

40 Bruno Latour, *The Politics of Nature*, trans. C. Porter (Cambridge, MA, 2004), p. 237.

41 Anthony Vidler, *Warped Space: Art, Architecture and Anxiety in Modern Culture* (Cambridge, MA, 2000), p. 67.

42 Harvie Ferguson, *Modernity and Subjectivity: Body, Soul, Spirit* (Charlottesville, VA, 2000), p. 45.

43 Geoff Ryman, *253* (London, 1998), p. 24.

44 Augé, *Non-places*, p. 78.

45 Kevin Lynch, *The Image of the City* (Cambridge, MA, 1960), p. 45.

46 Marc Atkins and Ian Sinclair, *Liquid City* (London, 1999).

47 Adrian Forty, *Objects of Desire: Design and Society since 1750* (London, 1986), p. 237.

48 Richard J. Williams, 'Pleasure and the Motorway', in *Autopia: Cars and Culture*, ed. Peter Wollen and Joe Kerr (London, 2002).

49 Vilém Flusser, 'On Memory (Electronic or Otherwise)', *Leonardo*, XXIII/4 (1990), p. 399.

50 Bruno Latour, 'A Cautious Prometheus? A Few Steps Toward a Philosophy of Design with Special Attention to Peter Sloterdijk', in *In Media Res: Peter Sloterdijk's Spherological Poetics of Being*, ed. Willem Schinkel and Liesbeth Noordegraaf-Eelens (Amsterdam, 2011), p. 158.

51 Nikolas Rose, 'Assembling the Modern Self', in *Rewriting the Self: Histories from the Renaissance to the Present*, ed. Roy Porter (London, 1997), pp. 239–40.

52 Michael Forrester, *Psychology of the Image* (London, 2000), p. 18.

53 Wendy Chun, 'The Enduring Ephemeral, or The Future is a Memory', *Critical Inquiry*, XXXV/1 (2008), p. 148.

54 Ibid., p. 154.

55 George Gilder, 'The Information Factories', *Wired* (October 2006).

56 Daniel Cossins, 'Digital Wonders of the World', *Wired* (November 2010).

57 Vernant, *Myth and Thought among the Greeks*, p. 428.

58 Jacques Le Goff, *History and Memory*, trans. Steven Rendall and
   Elizabeth Claman (New York, 1992), p. 63.

59 Flusser, 'On Memory (Electronic or Otherwise)', p. 399.

60 See 'Evernote and ios, Sittin' in a Tree', http://blog.evernote.com,
   24 May 2010.

61 Gordon Bell and Jim Gemmell, *Total Recall: How the E-Memory
   Revolution will Change Everything* (New York, 2009).

62 Ibid., p. 4.

63 Ibid.

64 R. U. Sirius, 'Out There Havin' Fun in the Warm Californian Sun', in
   Digital Delirium, ed. Arthur and Marilouise Kroker (Montreal, 2001),
   p. 13.

65 Michel Serres, *Genesis*, trans. Genevieve James and James Nielson
   (Ann Arbor, MI, 1995), p. 6.

66 Gilles Deleuze, *Negotiations, 1972–1990*, trans. Martin Joughin (New
   York, 1995), p. 121.

67 Tom Conley, 'Translator's Foreword', in Gilles Deleuze, *The Fold:
   Leibniz and the Baroque* (London and New York, 2006).

68 Description previously at www.ionaudio.com/products/details/
   twin-video (August 2012). See also Charlie Sorrel, 'Twin Video Puts
   Idiotic Operator in the Frame', www.wired.com, 21 January 2010.

69 Peter Sloterdijk, 'Foreword to the Theory of Spheres', in *Cosmograms*,
   ed. Melik Ohanian and Jean-Christophe Royoux (New York, 2004),
   p. 231.

70 G. W. Leibniz, 'New Essays on the Human Understanding', in
   Philosophical Writings, ed. G.H.R. Parkinson (London, 1973), p. 150.

71 Ibid.

72 The quotation is from Walter Benjamin, *The Arcades Project*, trans.
   Howard Eiland and Kevin McLaughlin (Cambridge, MA, 1999),
   p. 456.

73 Daniel Tiffany, *Infidel Poetics: Riddles, Nightlife, Substance* (Chicago,
   2009), p. 109.

74 Peter Sloterdijk, *Spheres*, vol. I: *Bubbles*, trans. Wieland Hoban (Los
   Angeles, CA, 2011), p. 498.

75 Hans Blumenberg, *Shipwreck with Spectator: Paradigm of a Metaphor
   for Existence*, trans. Steven Rendall (Cambridge, MA, 1997), p. 7.

76 Leibniz, 'New Essays on the Human Understanding', pp. 155–6.

77 Tiffany, *Infidel Poetics*, p. 103.

78 Michael Löwy, *Fire Alarm: Reading Walter Benjamin's 'On the
   Concept of History'*, trans. Chris Turner (London and New York,
   2005), p. 27.

79 Philip Fisher, *The Vehement Passions* (Princeton, NJ, 2003), p. 7.

80 Leibniz, 'New Essays on the Human Understanding', p. 157.

81 Daniel Heller-Roazen, *The Inner Touch: An Archaeology of Sensation* (New York, 2007), p. 194.
82 Press release by Nintendo for the new Wii console, 26 April 2006.
83 Roger Caillois, *Man, Play and Games*, trans. Meyer Barash (Urbana and Chicago, IL, 2001), pp. 23–4.
84 Hans Blumenberg, *Work on Myth*, trans. Robert M. Wallace (Cambridge, MA, 1985), p. 13.
85 Arthur Kroker and Michael A. Weinstein, *Data Trash: The Theory of the Virtual Class* (New York, 1994), p. 77.
86 Ibid.

Conclusion

1 Nikolas Rose, 'Assembling the Modern Self', in *Rewriting the Self: Histories from the Renaissance to the Present*, ed. Roy Porter (London, 1997), pp. 239–40.
2 Søren Kierkegaard, *Repetition*, trans. Walter Lowrie (Princeton, NJ, 1941), p. 35.
3 Jean-Pierre Vernant, *Myth and Thought among the Greeks*, trans. Janet Lloyd and Jeff Fort (New York, 2006), p. 429 n. 14.
4 On this point, see the discussion in Svetlana Boym, *The Future of Nostalgia* (New York, 2001), pp. 19–31.
5 Avery F. Gordon, *Ghostly Matters: Haunting and the Sociological Imagination* (Minneapolis, MN, 2008).
6 Fredric Jameson, *Postmodernism; or, The Cultural Logic of Late Capitalism* (London, 1991), p. ix.
7 Gaston Bachelard, 'The Hand Dreams: On Material Imagination', in Mary McAllester Jones, *Gaston Bachelard, Subversive Humanist: Texts and Readings* (Madison, WI, 1991), p. 104.
8 Randy Newman, *Sail Away* (Warner Bros. Records: Los Angeles, CA, 1972).

SELECT BIBLIOGRAPHY

Adorno, Theodor, and Max Horkheimer, *Dialectic of Enlightenment*,
    trans. John Cumming (London, 1997)
Agamben, Giorgio, *Potentialities: Collected Essays in Philosophy*, trans.
    Daniel Heller-Roazen (Stanford, CA, 1999)
Ankersmit, F. R., *History and Tropology: The Rise and Fall of Metaphor*
    (Berkeley, CA, 1994)
——, *Sublime Historical Experience* (Stanford, CA, 2005)
Assmann, Aleida, 'Texts, Traces, Trash: The Changing Media of Cultural
    Memory', *Representations*, LVI, Special Issue: 'The New Erudition'
    (Autumn 1996), pp. 123–34
Assmann, Jan, *Moses the Egyptian: The Memory of Egypt in Western
    Monotheism* (Cambridge, 1997)
Augé, Marc, *Non-places: Introduction to an Anthropology of
    Supermodernity*, trans. John Howe (London, 1995)
Barthes, Roland, *Camera Lucida*, trans. Richard Howard (London, 1993)
Benjamin, Walter, *The Arcades Project,* trans. Howard Eiland and Kevin
    McLaughlin (Cambridge, MA, 1999)
——, *Illuminations*, trans. Harry H. Zohn (London, 1994)
——, *One-way Street and Other Writings*, trans. Edmund Jephcott and
    Kingsley Shorter (London, 1997)
——, *Selected Writings*, vol. II, Part 1: *1927–1930*, trans. Rodney
    Livingstone et al. (Cambridge, MA, 1999)
——, *Selected Writings*, vol. III: *1935–1938*, trans. Edmund Jephcott,
    Howard Eiland et al. (Cambridge, MA, 2002)
——, *Walter Benjamin's Archive*, ed. Ursula Marx et al., trans. Esther Leslie
    (London and New York, 2007)
Berger, John, *The Camerawork Essays: Context and Meaning in
    Photography*, ed. Jessica Evans (London, 1997)
Bergson, Henri, *Matter and Memory*, trans. N. M. Paul and W. S. Palmer
    (New York, 1991)

Blumenberg, Hans, *The Legitimacy of the Modern Age*, trans. Robert
　　M. Wallace (Cambridge, MA, 1983)
——, *Shipwreck with Spectator: Paradigm of a Metaphor for Existence*,
　　trans. Steven Rendall (Cambridge, MA, 1997)
——, *Work on Myth*, trans. Robert M. Wallace (Cambridge, MA, 1985)
Boym, Svetlana, *The Future of Nostalgia* (New York, 2001)
Buck-Morss, Susan, *The Dialectics of Seeing: Walter Benjamin and the
　　Arcades Project* (Cambridge, MA, 1991)
Collingwood, R. G., *The Idea of History* [1946] (Oxford, 1961)
Derrida, Jacques, 'Plato's Pharmacy', in *Dissemination*, trans. Barbara
　　Johnson (London and New York, 2004), pp. 67–186
——, *Points . . . Interviews, 1974–1994*, trans. Peggy Kamuf et al.
　　(Stanford, CA, 1995)
Durkheim, Emile, *The Elementary Forms of Religious Life*, trans. John
　　Ward Swain (New York, 2008)
Eliade, Mircea, *Myth and Reality*, trans. Willard R. Trask (New York and
　　Evanston, IL, 1963)
Ferguson, Harvie, *Self-identity and Everyday Life* (London, 2009)
Fisher, Philip, *The Vehement Passions* (Princeton, NJ, 2003)
Flusser, Vilém, 'On Memory (Electronic or Otherwise)', *Leonardo*, XXIII/4
　　(1990), pp. 397–9
Freud, Sigmund, 'Preface to Reik's *Ritual: Psycho-Analytic Studies*', in
　　The Standard Edition of the Complete Psychological Works trans.
　　J. Strachey (London, 1955), vol. XVII, pp. 257–64
——, 'Remembering, Repeating and Working Through', in *The Standard
　　Edition of the Complete Psychological Works*, trans. J. Strachey
　　(London, 1955), vol. VI, pp. 274–5
Ginzburg, Carlo, *The Cheese and the Worms: The Cosmos of a Sixteenth-
　　century Miller*, trans. John and Ann C. Tedeschi (Baltimore, MD,
　　1992)
——, *Clues, Myths and the Historical Method*, trans. John and Ann
　　C. Tedeschi (Baltimore, MD, 1989)
——, 'Minutiae, Close-up, Microanalysis', *Critical Inquiry*, XXXIV/1
　　(Autumn 2007), pp. 174–89
——, *Wooden Eyes: Nine Reflections on Distance*, trans. Martin Ryle and
　　Kate Soper (New York, 2001)
Harrison, Robert Pogue, *The Dominion of the Dead* (Chicago, 2003)
Hegel, G.W.F., *Phenomenology of Spirit*, trans. A. V. Miller (Oxford, 1977)
Homer, *The Odyssey*, trans. E. V. Rieu and D.C.H. Rieu (London, 1991)
Halbwachs, Maurice, *The Collective Memory*, trans. Francis J. Ditter Jr and
　　Vida Yazdi Ditter (New York, 1980)
——, *On Collective Memory*, ed. and trans. with an introduction by Lewis
　　A. Coser (Chicago and London, 1992)

Jameson, Fredric, 'The End of Temporality', *Critical Inquiry*, XXIX/4 (2003), pp. 695–718

——, *The Seeds of Time* (New York, 1994)

Jay, Martin, *Downcast Eyes: The Denigration of Vision in Twentieth-century French Thought* (Berkeley, CA, 1993)

——, *Songs of Experience: Modern American and European Variations on a Universal Theme* (Berkeley, CA, 2005)

Kittler, Friedrich, *Gramophone, Film, Typewriter*, trans. Geoffrey Winthrop-Young and Michael Wutz (Stanford, CA, 1999)

Kracauer, Siegfried, 'On the Writings of Walter Benjamin', in *The Mass Ornament: Weimar Essays*, trans. Thomas Y. Levin (Cambridge, MA, 1995), pp. 259–66

LaBelle, Brandon, *Background Noise: Perspectives on Sound Art* (London, 2006)

Landy, Joshua, *Philosophy as Fiction: Self, Deception and Knowledge in Proust* (Oxford, 2004)

Le Goff, Jacques, *History and Memory*, trans. Steven Rendall and Elizabeth Claman (New York, 1992)

Leibniz, G. W., *Philosophical Writings*, ed. G.H.R. Parkinson (London, 1973)

Locke, John, *Essay Concerning Human Understanding*, abridged and ed. with an introduction by John W. Yolton (London, 1976)

Löwy, Michael, *Fire Alarm: Reading Walter Benjamin's 'On the Concept of History'*, trans. Chris Turner (London and New York, 2005)

Nancy, Jean-Luc, *Hegel: The Restlessness of the Negative*, trans. Jason Smith and Steven Miller (Minneapolis, MN, 2002)

Nietzsche, Friedrich, *Beyond Good and Evil*, trans. R. Hollingdale (London, 2003)

——, *Untimely Meditations*, trans. R. Hollingdale (Cambridge, 1997)

Nora, Pierre, 'Between Memory and History: *Les Lieux de mémoire*', trans. Marc Roudebush, *Representations*, XXVI (1989), pp. 7–24

——, 'General Introduction: Between Memory and History', in *Realms of Memory: Rethinking the French Past*, vol. I, trans. Arthur Goldhammer (New York, 1996), pp. 1–20

Pippin, Robert, *The Persistence of Subjectivity: On the Kantian Aftermath* (Cambridge, 2005)

Plato, *Phaedrus*, trans. Robert Waterfield (Oxford, 2002)

Porter, Roy, ed., *Rewriting the Self: Histories from the Renaissance to the Present* (London, 1997)

Proust, Marcel, *In Search of Lost Time*, vol. I: *Swann's Way*, trans. C. K. Scott Moncrieff and Terence Kilmartin, revd D. J. Enright (London, 1996)

Ricoeur, Paul, *Memory, History, Forgetting*, trans. Kathleen Blamey and

David Pellauer (Chicago, 2004)

Rohde, Erwin, *Psyche: The Cult of Souls and Belief in Immortality Among the Greeks*, trans. from the 8th edn by W. B. Hillis (London, 1925)

Samuel, Raphael, *Theatres of Memory*, vol. I: *Past and Present in Contemporary Culture* (London, 1994)

Santner, Eric L., *On Creaturely Life: Rilke, Benjamin, Sebald* (Chicago, 2006)

Schama, Simon, *Landscape and Memory* (London, 1995)

Schwartz, Lynne Sharon, ed., *The Emergence of Memory: Conversations with W. G. Sebald* (New York, 2007)

Sebald, W. G., *The Emigrants*, trans. Michael Hulse (London, 2002)

Seigel, Jerrold, *The Idea of the Self: Thought and Experience in Western Europe since the Seventeenth Century* (Cambridge, 2005)

Serres, Michel, *Genesis*, trans. Genevieve James and James Nielson (Ann Arbor, MI, 1995)

Sloterdijk, Peter, *Spheres*, vol. I: *Bubbles*, trans. Wieland Hoban (Los Angeles, CA, 2011)

Sontag, Susan, *On Photography* (London, 1978)

Thompson, Emily, *The Soundscape of Modernity: Architectural Acoustics and the Culture of Listening in America, 1900–1933* (Cambridge, MA, 2002)

Tiffany, Daniel, *Infidel Poetics: Riddles, Nightlife, Substance* (Chicago, 2009)

Vernant, Jean-Pierre, *Myth and Society in Ancient Greece*, trans. Janet Lloyd (New York, 1988)

——, *Myth and Thought among the Greeks*, trans. Janet Lloyd and Jeff Fort (New York, 2006)

Warner, Marina, *Fantastic Metamorphoses, Other Worlds* (Oxford, 2002)

Yates, Frances A., *The Art of Memory* (London, 2002)

ACKNOWLEDGEMENTS

This book was first conceived in 2006–7, around the time I began working in the Department of Sociology at the University of Bristol. Thanks largely to my then head of department, Ruth Levitas – who allowed me to develop a teaching module on memory – I was allowed to indulge my developing research interests in this area. For similar reasons, I would like also to acknowledge the support of Maria Wowk at Manchester Metropolitan University, who gave me an opportunity to further develop my teaching on the subject over the last three years, and in so doing allowed me some space to think through ideas that emerge in the book. I am grateful to Michael Leaman at Reaktion Books for his patience, and to Aimee Selby, my exceptionally perceptive editor, whose close reading and demands for clarification in the final stages no doubt have helped improve this book. I should also mention the help and support of some colleagues during the period when I have been writing this book: Heather Burroughs for – as ever – proffering the kind of wisdom that when taken (usually) prevents me from making much worse decisions than I already make; Annie Meyer, for always raising the spirits at work, and for countless lifts home – even on those occasions when I ended up the victim of a passenger seat that seemed to belong in a Chaplin sketch about autonomous machinery; and Colin Wisely, for showing me how Odysseus would change the wheel on a car, and also for alerting me to the 'Historical Enquiries Team', which I discuss in chapter Three.

My greatest debt of gratitude, however, is to Harvie Ferguson, who has been a source of moral and intellectual support for many years. Many of the ideas in this book relating to what I describe as 'Surf Life' emerged out of discussions with Harvie Ferguson that were drawn out over a fairly long period of time. Sometime around 2006 or 2007 we began to think of what we would then often refer to simply as 'Surf' as a means of comprehending the importance of feeling and emotion in the life of contemporary Western societies. This image/metaphor, he eventually persuaded me, was distinct from ideas of flows, or liquidity (which by then already had a fairly longstanding sociological currency): 'Surf' suggested, rather, a breaking wave whose particles dissolve into the atmosphere. We felt that in a good deal of contemporary 'experience' the traditional sociological concerns with subject (agency) and object (structure) distinctions no longer provided a viable means of accounting for the ways in which people live; rather, it seemed evident that in numerous aspects of everyday life subject and object merge and dissolve repeatedly, and that self-identity is not as fixed as a notion like 'experience' traditionally suggested, but has many momentary states. I have attempted to explore this Surf Life as it relates to memory, particularly in terms of thinking of memory in 'ecological' terms (that is, in terms that transcend subject–object distinctions). This puts the focus more particularly on how we can understand memory to be about the importance of a number of ideas that are linked to how we conceive of our home in this world (as, variously, homeland, habitat and 'interior'). The precursors to Surf Life, intellectually speaking, can be found in numerous sources that are acknowledged in the book itself; but, in publication terms, Surf Life – even if not explicitly the subject – had already crept into earlier work. Harvie Ferguson's elaboration of the fragmentary and 'selfless non-identity' of everyday life (in *Self-Identity and Everyday Life*, 2009) provides a theoretical background to Surf Life that puts it more securely within the context of modern thought, and the development of sociology more particularly; and my book *Van Halen: Exuberant California, Zen Rock'n'Roll* (2012) offers, in part, a case study of Surf Life through a consideration of the aesthetics of a rock band that, in creative and performance terms, sought something other than the self-expression that is typically lauded as proof of cultural 'authenticity' by scholars of popular music – they sought, rather, a kind of *awareness* or *receptivity* to their environment that would purposively efface subject–object distinctions.

PHOTO ACKNOWLEDGEMENTS

The author and publishers wish to express their thanks to the below sources of illustrative material and/or permission to reproduce it:

Author's collection: p. 8; from Francis Bacon, *Instauratio magna* (London, 1620): p. 22; Corbis: pp. 45, 149; Dreamstime: pp. 28, 113, 123; courtesy English Heritage: p. 47; from A. Ganot, *Natural Philosophy for General Readers and Young Persons* (New York, 1872): p. 65; Getty Images: pp. 82, 101; Katsushika Hokusai, 'The Great Wave off Kanagawa', woodblock print, *c.* 1829–32, from the series *Thirty-six Views of Mount Fuji*, 1826–33: p. 149; Library of Congress, Washington, DC: p. 89.

INDEX

Adorno, Theodor 20, 24
Agamben, Giorgio 118
alethia (Gr. 'unforgetting') 30
Alzheimer's disease 14
amnesia 13–15, 118, 121, 124, 130, 132, 154
'amnesty' (forgiveness), relation to amnesia 118
anamnesis 11, 23, 28–9, 118, 129, 145, 149
Ankersmit, Frank 30, 33, 36, 38, 39
Apple computer 140–41, 152
archives 7, 10, 45, 63, 67, 74, 76, 87, 88, 90, 108, 121, 134, 138, 139, 142, 143
Aristotle 12, 14, 143
'artificial memory' 90–91
Asendorf, Christoph 78
Assmann, Aleida 97
Assmann, Jan 113, 116
Augé, Marc 122, 127
autobiography 12–13, 46, 52, 80

Bacon, Francis 22, 32, 33
Barthes, Roland 78–9, 80–81
Baudelaire, Charles 58, 77–8, 85, 110, 127
Beatles, The 98
Benjamin, Walter 10–12, 17, 19, 20, 39, 51–60, 76–80, 82–5, 87, 88, 91–3, 97–102, 104–5, 107, 112, 131, 146, 149–50
Berger, John 67, 68

Bergson, Henri 61, 62, 63, 68, 69, 73, 114
Berman, Marshall 27
Blow-Up (film, Michelangelo Antonioni) 83–5, *85*, 103, 121
Blumenberg, Hans 22, 24, 29, 147, 149
Borges, Jorge Luis 67, 104, 105
Boyer, M. Christine 46
Boym, Svetlana 21
Buci-Glucksmann, Christine 58
Buck-Morss, Susan 54, 56

Caillois, Roger 152
camera obscura 64, *65*, 76
Carruthers, Mary 91
Caruth, Cathy 120
childhood 11, 14, 26, 49–56, 59, 63, 80, 114, 116, 123, 140, 155, 156
collective memory 31, 39, 68, 109, 110, 150
    Walter Benjamin 11–12, 54, 59, 77, 85, 91, 107, 112
    Maurice Halbwachs 112, 114–21
    and networks 129–31, 133
    Aby Warburg 112
Collingwood, R. G. 32–5
conscience collective ('collective conscious', Emile Durkheim) 109–12, 118, 119, 120
Corbin, Alain 93–4, 110

'Dayton, Ohio, 1913' (song, Randy Newman) 158
death (awareness of as condition of memory) 15, 18, 23, 50, 58, 61, 70, 73, 78–81, 92, 102, 111, 141, 144, 148
déjà vu 10, 62
Deleuze, Gilles 69, 122, 128, 142
Derrida, Jacques 73–4, 95–7
Descartes 64–6, 68, 114, 115, 132
dialectical image (Walter Benjamin) 99–101, 146
Dick, Philip K. 71
Diderot, Denis 12
digital heritage conservation 135–6
digital life 7–8, 132, 133, 134–43, 146, 150–51, 153
Duchamp, Marcel 38
Durkheim, Emile 109–12, 114–17, 120, 133

Edensor, Tim 46
Edison, Thomas 89
Elgin Marbles 28
Eliade, Mircea 110
Evernote (mobile app) 137

Ferguson, Harvie 24, 106, 108, 126
Fisher, Philip 13, 150
Flusser, Vilém 137
Forty, Adrian 130
Fox Talbot, William Henry 63, 75, 76, 79
Freud, Sigmund 35, 39, 57, 69, 98, 110, 120, 121

Georgics (Virgil) 103
Gibbon, Edward 29
Ginzburg, Carlo 35–40, 53

habit 15, 36, 44, 45, 68, 73, 76, 95, 105, 110, 111, 112, 121–5, 127–31, 135, 138, 157, 158
habitat 15–16, 18, 42, 50, 69, 121, 135, 140–44, 148–52
Hacking, Ian 14

Halbwachs, Maurice 68, 112, 114–17, 131
Harootunian, Harry 56
Harrison, Robert 18
Hegel, G.W.F. 24, 25, 26, 27, 120
Heidegger, Martin 18
herbal memory supplements 8, 8
heritage culture 28, 28, 29, 40–45, 45, 46, 47, 70, 109, 135
Highmore, Ben 100
Historical Enquiries Team (Northern Ireland) 118–19, 120–21
historical experience and modernity 10, 26, 27, 53–4, 56, 58, 126
historical re-enactment 45
history
    historiography 26, 27, 28, 29, 30
    and microhistory (Ginzburg) 35–9
    in Friedrich Nietzsche 42–3
    and truth 32–5
home, idea of 9–10, 15–21, 23, 25–6, 28, 30, 32, 43, 49–51, 53–4, 55, 67, 69, 86, 93, 111, 114, 117, 120, 122, 128–9, 132, 134, 140, 143–4, 146–7, 148–9, 150, 156
homesickness 9–10, 24, 25–6, 28, 30, 54, 117
Horkheimer, Max 20, 24

identity 13, 14, 17, 24, 25, 26, 74, 77, 105–6, 131, 137, 144, 147
    see also self-identity
'image of the city' (Kevin Lynch) 129
images (mental) 49, 51–2, 56–9, 60–69, 70–71, 74–9, 100–01, 116–18, 126, 127, 128, 129, 130–31, 143, 155
involuntary memory 9, 38, 50, 56, 57, 60, 63, 70, 75, 77, 78, 81, 88

Jameson, Fredric 19, 107, 157
Jobs, Steve 140
Johnson, Samuel 87–8

Katsushika Hokusai, The Great Wave off Kanagawa 149

Kennedy, John F. (Zapruder film of assassination) 86
Kierkegaard, Søren 155
Kircher, Athanasius 76
Kittler, Friedrich 51, 61, 88–9, 90, 98
Koyaanisqatsi (film, Godfrey Reggio) 128–9, 129
Kracauer, Siegfried 53, 57

Landy, Joshua 63
language and culture 18, 31, 68, 102–3, 111, 116, 119, 122
Latour, Bruno 125, 133
Le Goff, Jacques 33, 34
Leeming, David Adams 109, 115
Leibniz, Gottfried Wilhelm 11, 35, 36, 39, 53, 57, 60, 123, 145–6, 148–51
Lenson, David 73
Lethe (river of forgetting) 15, 157
lieux de mémoire 31, 35, 44–5, 63, 74
    see also Nora, Pierre
life-logging 138–9
Locke, John 12–13, 42, 64, 103, 143, 145–6
Lowenthal, David 35, 41, 46

magnetic tape 92, 99–100, 102, 104
maps 128–30
Marx, Karl 26
Mellor, David Allen 86
memorials 42, 74, 113
'memory pills' see herbal memory supplements
microhistory (Carlo Ginzburg) 35–9
Mill, John Stuart 30
Minority Report (film, Steven Spielberg) 71–3
mnemon (ancient Greece) 136–7
mnemonics 119, 121, 122
Mnemosyne
    as personification of memory 29, 120
    as river in Homeric myth 15
modernity
    as self-consciousness 17–27, 58, 76–7

and time 19, 24, 29, 45, 54, 56–8, 66, 77, 78, 81, 88, 91, 93, 100, 101, 109
and tradition 19, 27–32, 44–5, 49, 58, 77, 92, 93, 109–19, 147, 156
    see also history
monadic existence 126, 149–51
monadological thinking
    Walter Benjamin 11, 53, 146, 149
    Carlo Ginzburg 35–6, 38–9, 53
monadology (G. W. Leibniz, theory of monads) 145–6, 148
'Monadology' (essay, G. W. Leibniz) 35, 146, 149
Montaigne, Michel de 12
Moorman, Mary 86
Museum of Me (Intel/Facebook) 139
museums 28, 45, 46, 48, 74, 139
musique concrète 99, 100, 102
My Life in the Bush of Ghosts (album, Brian Eno and David Byrne) 102–6
'My Sweet Lord' (song, George Harrison) 49

Nancy, Jean-Luc 26
networks 122–31, 133, 140–42, 146
new media 70, 106, 107–8
Nietzsche, Friedrich 9, 15, 19, 40, 41, 42, 43, 48, 119
Nora, Pierre 31, 35, 44, 46, 63, 74
nostalgia 10, 19, 20–21, 24, 28, 30, 49, 54, 69, 74, 117, 148, 156–7
Novalis (Georg Philipp Friedrich von Hardenberg) 9, 18, 109

Odysseus (Ulysses) 19–26, 28–9, 70–72, 147
Odyssey (Homer) 20–21, 26, 69–70, 72, 73

Pamerleau, William 85
philosophical toys 66
phonograph 69, 89, 89, 90
phonography and writing 94–7
photography 60–69, 70–71, 74–5, 76–9, 88, 97, 137
    and unconscious optics 81–7

Pick, Daniel 66
'plane of immanence' (Gilles
    Deleuze and Félix Guattari) 122,
    123, 128
Plato 11, 29, 57, 61, 63, 64, 94, 95,
    102, 145
play 150–52
Poovey, Mary 87
'postmemory' 74
Proust, Marcel 8, 13, 41, 50, 56, 60,
    62–3, 73, 75, 77–8

Reich, Steve 100, 102
repetition 73–4, 91, 94, 96, 99, 105,
    110, 117, 124, 129, 131, 156
    see also habit
Richter, Gerhard 98
Ricoeur, Paul 15, 31, 39, 60–61
Rose, Nikolas 133, 155
Ryman, Geoff 126

Samuel, Raphael 43–4, 79, 109
Santner, Eric L. 58
Schaeffer, Pierre 99–101, 101
Schama, Simon 35, 43
Scholem, Gershom 59
Schwartz, Hillel 73
Schwitters, Kurt 100
Sebald, W. G. 46–8, 71
Second World War 44, 46, 83, 109
self-consciousness 9, 15, 18, 24–6, 28,
    29, 31, 50, 63, 111, 156
self-identity 13–14, 25, 144, 147
'self-image'
    as memory (Proust) 77
    Emile Durkheim 111, 114, 116
Serres, Michel 93, 104–5, 141
Simmel, Georg 126
Sirens (in Homeric myth) 21, 23
Sirius, R. U. 139
Sloterdijk, Peter 21, 50, 143, 147
Socrates (in Plato, Phaedrus) 94–7
Sontag, Susan 75–6, 78
soul, the
    as monad in Leibniz 150
    as seat of memory 11, 14, 23,
        61, 145

as 'image' or 'shade' in Homeric
    myth 70
sound
    as phenomenon 88–9, 92–108
    phonographic 89, 92–108
    'surf' (metaphor elaborated) 11,
        141–2, 150
    see also 'Surf Life'
'Surf Life' 11, 106, 121, 127, 140–54
'surfacing' 128, 130, 137, 141, 142
surfeit
    of 'memory' 40, 42, 48, 141–2
    'too-muchness' of reality 11, 56,
        87–8, 94, 121, 142

Thompson, Emily 88, 92
Tiffany, Daniel 148
Tönnies, Ferdinand 26
Toop, David 98
trauma (and the past) 17, 54–7, 72,
    109–19, 120–21, 155
Truth and Reconciliation
    Commission (South Africa) 121

unconscious, the
    auditory unconscious 98, 100,
        102–5
    Bergson and 61
    Freudian 57, 98
    Leibniz and 57, 148, 150–52
    the past as (Ginzburg) 35–6, 38–9
    the past as (Benjamin) 51–2, 55,
        56, 57, 58, 77
    the past as (Sebald) 71
    recollection and 9, 11, 13, 17, 26,
        35, 42, 47, 50, 51, 115, 158
    'unconscious optics' (Benjamin)
        39, 81, 82, 83, 84, 85, 86, 97,
        103
    as the underworld in Homeric
        myth 69–70, 71
    see also involuntary memory

Vattimo, Gianni 115
Vernant, Jean-Pierre 15, 28, 29, 103,
    136, 156
Vidler, Anthony 126

virtual, the
  memory as realm of 9, 40–41,
    68–70, 72–3, 90
  virtual space 133–4, 139
  virtual technologies 7, 107, 137,
    152–4
  see also digital life

Warner, Marina 76
Wittgenstein, Ludwig 56

writing
  and inscription 63, 87–8, 90–91,
    94–5, 97–8, 101–2, 107, 136,
    137, 143
  as narcosis (Derrida) 94–7

Yates, Frances A. 90–91

Zapruder, Abraham 86–7
Zielinski, Siegfried 86